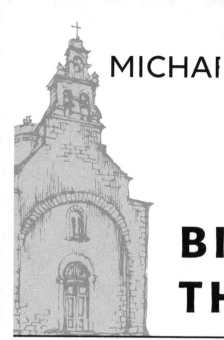

MICHAEL

A
BIBLICAL
THEOLOGY

of

YOUTH
MINISTRY

TEENAGERS IN THE LIFE OF THE CHURCH

FOREWORD BY WALT MUELLER

RANDALL HOUSE
— ACADEMIC —

114 Bush Rd | Nashville, TN 37217
randallhouse.com

For Tracy
I'd choose you all over again

For Matthew and Hannah
Being your dad is my greatest accomplishment

TABLE OF CONTENTS

Acknowledgements

As with all books, this would have been impossible without the support and encouragement of many people. First and foremost is my family. Tracy, your loving support has made this possible. Your work with teenagers in the public school is genuine ministry and your passion for education inspires me daily. To Matthew and Hannah, my greatest prayer for you both is that you would remember our family motto and continue to love God, love others, and be gummy.

Thank you to Charles Cook and Michelle Orr and the rest of the team at Randall House Academic for believing in this project. To Chris Talbot, your kindness and help was instrumental. To my mentors in ministry, thank you. Craig Secor, Walt Mueller, Duffy Robbins, Adonis Vidu, Mark Cannister, Bob Whittet — your fingerprints can be seen throughout the pages of this book. Thanks to my long-time friends who have held me up, Dan Sylvia and Mike Mura.

The Rooted Ministry has undeniably changed my life as I have walked this journey of gospel-centered youth ministry. Attending the Rooted Conference was the first time I felt like I was among youth pastors who truly understood me. With all the contemporary talk of the Pastor-Theologian making a comeback, my Rooted family has shown me that it is also possible to be a Youth Pastor-Theologian.

Finally, thank you to my church family at Emmanuel Baptist Church in Norfolk, Massachusetts. I especially want to thank those who have served with me in the youth ministry over the years – Trisha, Andrew, Alyson, Keith, Andy, Mark, Kevin, Josh, Cait, Michele, Wes, Mark, Gayle, and Wayne. To all the parents of students, thank you for your patience, support. May EBC continue to develop as a Bridge Building Church where parents and youth workers truly co-evangelize and co-disciple the next generation.

Foreword

by Walt Mueller

I recently heard a long-time youth ministry leader share this observation: "Most youth workers I know aren't asking the question 'What should I believe?' Rather, most youth workers are asking the question 'What should I do?'"

The observation is spot on. It's also alarming.

I'm alarmed on a personal level due to my own youth ministry history. When I launched into what's now become my 40 years in the youth ministry world, my approach was far too pragmatic. Rather than first taking the time to ponder the more serious foundational theological questions that could have and should have informed my ministry practice, I quickly skipped that step (albeit unknowingly) and defaulted into the pragmatic. After all, I had youth ministry work *to do*. What I *did* in those early years, I'm embarrassed to say, was "program for growth." While I would have told you that my concept of "growth" was seeing evidence of young people moving toward maturity in Christ, my look in the rear-view-mirror forces me to be honest with myself. Truth be told, the growth I shot for was "bigger and better" in terms of measurable metrics. I believed we were on the mark when others commented on how "vibrant and active!" our youth group had become. But if I had taken the time to dig deeper, I would have discovered that it would have only taken one shovel full of dirt to reach the shallows to which I was leading kids.

Now that I've had a chance to evaluate my own youth ministry history through the lens of what I hope is a more balanced, wise, theologically-informed, and spiritually mature understanding of youth ministry, I'm deeply concerned that while the cultural surroundings and challenges have changed, we're still doing youth ministry in ways that not only shoot at the wrong target, but result in attendance and activity largely void of theological reflection and the resulting deep spiritual growth. And sadly, we now function in a church culture that increasingly embraces a pragmatism that values metrics while de-valuing the importance of conscious, biblically-faithful, theological reflection, which results in God-glorifying and Kingdom-expanding praxis.

Based on what I read in the Scriptures combined with my own experience, I am now passionate about telling youth workers that theology *is not* optional. Whether it is consciously pursued or unconsciously ignored, theology is always at the foundation of our ministry strategies and practices. If we take the time to engage in good theological reflection, we will be able to articulate the beliefs that inform our ministry practices and behaviors. But if we ignore the necessary step of theological reflection, our strategies and praxis will simply happen. Most likely, our efforts—however well-intentioned they may be—won't result in outcomes marked by faithfulness to God's will and way for ministry. I believe this is at the root of the documented decline in spiritual maturity, as well as the continuing exodus of young adults from the church as they graduate from youth group and home, and move into the independence of adult life.

I am a firm believer in the fact that youth ministry holds a valuable place in the life of the church. I also believe that youth ministry is an endeavor that should support rather than supplant the primary role of parents to nurture their children in the faith. And, I believe that conscious, biblically-faithful theological reflection must be pursued passionately and without pause by those called to engage in this wonderful endeavor we call youth ministry!

Over the course of the last decade, I've been encouraged by the growing number of youth workers, churches, and families who are investing in the lives of kids by thinking theologically about youth ministry. I've walked with Mike McGarry as together we've worked as a part of a group of people determined to first seek answers to the "What should I believe?" question as a necessary and foundational first step before asking "What should I do?" As a practitioner, Mike continues to ask himself the hard questions that must be asked. I'm grateful he's doing some of the heavy exegetical and theological lifting in ways that will benefit us all…especially our kids, as we labor to help them understand and embrace the gospel!

This book will serve our youth ministry community well. For those who are just now embarking on their youth ministry journey, Mike provides a biblical/theological foundation on which to build faithful praxis. For those who have been on the youth ministry journey for some time, Mike offers a theological perspective that will serve to help you evaluate the foundations and direction of your ministry in ways I hope will lead to both affirmations and course corrections.

Introduction:
Why This Book is Necessary

When I was in junior high, my parents were navigating a separation, which eventually led to divorce. My church had recently called a new youth pastor. He was old. Well, we thought he was, although he was probably late-thirties at the time. When Craig and his family arrived, my mom and I were among the first there to greet him and his family, then we helped move boxes into his house. I had no idea at the time, but Craig would later play a pivotal role in my life. He would be the one who helped me come to terms with my parents' divorce, challenge me to teach my first Bible study, and later create an opportunity for me to serve as his intern for two years during college.

Like many former youth group students, my tendency is to re-create the youth group experience I had as a teenager. But when I consider the other teenagers who went to youth group with me, the statistics bring me pause. Many (most?) of those who attended youth group with me are no longer walking with Christ. Between this and my own experience as the Pastor of Youth & Families for thirteen years there can be a gnawing feeling that, "This isn't working!" Reports about the futility of youth ministry have caused me (and most other youth workers) much grief. After all, what if the critics are right? What if we aren't merely wasting our time, but actually contributing to the problem? These are the secret concerns many youth workers share.

The statistics about the "dropout rate" are not mere numbers to us, but students whom we have known and served and loved in the name of Christ. Their faces come to mind whenever we think about the joys and the trials of ministry. Some former-students who came from unbelieving homes and are still walking faithfully with Christ into adulthood, bearing witness to a true and lasting conversion. Others were raised by faithful Christian parents yet reject their childhood faith. We often find ourselves surprised by whose faith remains and whose has withered, but we endure in ministry, trusting the Lord to reserve a remnant for Himself among a seemingly lost generation.

Youth ministry has begun a shift over the past decade. An increasing number of leaders has considered the "dropout rate" and started asking difficult questions about the validity and practice of youth ministry. They raise many of the same concerns youth workers have discussed and debated among one another, but they broaden the discussion beyond youth workers. This has set the stage for a new era of youth ministry, where the entire church is being called to renew its commitment to the next generation and to family discipleship. As youth ministry continues to transition into a new era marked by a renewed emphasis on ministry to parents and integration of youth into the life of the church, we must consider the foundations.

Some critics, particularly those from the Family Integrated Church Movement, call into question whether or not youth ministry is biblical at all. Voddie Baucham provocatively states, "There is no clear biblical mandate for the current approach [to youth ministry]."[1] While there are modern youth ministry paradigms that are unbiblical, he continues by questioning the validity of youth ministry entirely, "...I have been invited to lecture in youth ministry classes in colleges and seminaries over the past several years. However, what I have never had is a conver-

---

[1] Voddie Baucham, *Family Driven Faith: Doing What It Takes to Raise Sons and Daughters Who Walk With God* (Wheaton, IL: Crossway Books, 2011), 185.

sation with a person presenting the argument for segregated youth/children's ministry from an open Bible. I have never had a professor, a student, a youth pastor, or anyone else show me book, chapter, and verse in defense of the contemporary model."[2] Scott Brown has written that youth ministry is "a weed in the church" that should not be reformed, but uprooted.[3] While their solutions are less than convincing, they ask legitimate and serious questions that should be considered.

- Is youth ministry biblical?
- Have we been doing youth ministry in a way that has produced short-term "results" but, in the long-term, feeds into the dropout rate?
- Are we so reliant on pragmatism and "what works" that we have forsaken biblical teaching about evangelism and discipleship?
- Why do so many Christian families off-load their children's discipleship to workers in the church while neglecting their biblical calling to instruct their children?
- Is the local church structured and programmed in a way that silently encourages this parental negligence?

The purpose of *A Biblical Theology of Youth Ministry: Teenagers in the Life of the Church* is to address these questions by presenting a biblical, historical, and theological foundation for youth ministry. This is not intended to be a handbook or a new ministry paradigm. Instead, the emphasis of this book is on presenting a clear and simple but thoroughly biblical framework for thinking about youth ministry as the church's expression of partnership with the family for co-evangelizing and co-discipling the next generation. The closing chapter will present some practical guidance based off these foundations.

---

[2]Ibid.

[3]Scott T. Brown, *A Weed in the Church*, (Wake Forest, NC: The National Center for Family-Integrated Churches, 2011).

The following represents the overarching argument of this book. Exploring the Old Testament's calling to pass on the faith to the next generation provides a clear example that while parents are the primary disciple-makers of their children, the entire community was implicitly responsible. In the New Testament, we see examples through Jesus' ministry to the apostles (who were all unmarried men except for Peter) and in certain commands about the older believers training the younger within the family of faith. Understanding the journey of new converts throughout Church History sheds light on those who might be considered the Church's first youth workers: catechists who would teach and prepare "church kids" for baptism or confirmation. The theological nature of the family and of the church set the entire discussion about the viability of youth ministry into a broader framework within the church's longstanding approach toward the next generation. Finally, the gospel is the proclamation of the saving grace of God to sinners who believe on Christ for salvation, and this is to be the driving center of all aspects of Christian life and ministry.

As the next generation of youth workers proclaim the gospel and disciple students, they must do so upon a solid foundation. They must resist the temptation to merely repeat what they themselves experienced and turn back to Scripture for guidance. It is time for the whole church to get involved, for parents to be equipped, and for youth workers to see themselves as a bridge between the church and home. Youth ministry is for adolescence, the family is for life, but the Church is for eternity. May youth workers lead and serve accordingly.

Chapter 1

The Landscape of Modern Youth Ministry

There comes a point in every youth pastor's ministry when he or she fearfully sits back and asks, "Am I doing this right?" This may happen after his or her first year when well-crafted plans get disrupted by uncooperative youth leaders. Perhaps students are simply not responding to ministry initiatives in expected ways. Often, this question plagues youth workers after their first decade of ministry and they reflect on faithful students who have walked away from the faith while other students have surprisingly continued in faithfulness. Many youth workers are beginning to conclude, "I don't think I'd be doing things this way if I was starting over from scratch, with just the Bible and Church History to guide me." This book is for aspiring youth workers as well as for veterans who are reconsidering the biblical, historical, and theological foundations for youth ministry. There are surprisingly few books that build a foundation for youth ministry through exegetical and theological study.

Before exploring the biblical, historical, and theological foundations of youth ministry, it is important to get an accurate picture of the landscape of modern youth ministry.

Three Foundational Problems Facing Modern Youth Ministry

There are three foundational problems facing youth ministry that youth workers have long discussed but must also be addressed with church leaders and parents. First, one must understand the "dropout rate," which is often cited as a description of how many students stop attending church after graduating high school. Second, it is important to recognize that youth culture reflects a broader problem—it is not exclusively youth who are dropping out of church-involvement. American culture as a whole is becoming increasingly non-Christian, and the problem of youth abandoning their faith reflects the same trend among adults. Third, in many churches there is a fragmentation between the church, the youth ministry, and the family. These problems converge to create a recipe whereby the second and third problems continue to fuel the first.

The Dropout Rate

It is no secret that the American Church is in a time of crisis regarding the emerging generation.[4] It is well known that the majority of church-attending teenagers abandon their faith after high school. Many studies have been done to determine what the actual dropout rate is, but it seems they have only proven that a reliable and clear-cut statistic is likely impossible to determine. Most recently, Lifeway Research has reported, "66 percent of students who were active in their church during high school no longer remained active in the church between ages 18-22."[5] This finding is 4% better than the 70% dropout rate Lifeway identified when they conducted the same research in

---

[4]This includes all those who are between 12-21 years old. While many adolescent theorists today agree that "adolescence" may stretch well into one's twenties, I will limit this term to those who are most clearly "not yet adults."

[5]Ben Trueblood, *Within Reach: The Power of Small Changes in Keeping Students Connected* (Nashville, TN: Lifeway, 2018), 12.

2007. Despite that improvement, it is doubtful any parent or pastor would be willing to knowingly sacrifice two-thirds of the students in his or her youth ministry without great anguish and many tears. The best-case scenario remains eternally tragic.

While many churches are tempted to remedy this tragedy with more attractive programs and an endless search for "relevance." Considering the undeniable influence parents have on a teenager's spirituality, perhaps a wiser approach would be to empower parents and strengthen the homes in which today's teenagers are being raised. On the surface, this may not be as impressive as a large youth ministry with all the bells and whistles, but it will surely make a greater long-term impact. As both local churches and families both continue to crumble into disarray and are in a period of genuine crisis, more programs are not the solution. The Church must recommit herself to the gospel and to discipleship to strengthen an inner core whereby families may then be strengthened.

The Barna Group has done extensive research on how parents view their spiritual responsibility to their children, concluding, "Close to nine out of ten parents of children under age 13 believe they have the primary responsibility for teaching their children about religious beliefs and spiritual matters. ... Related research, however, revealed that a majority of parents do not spend any time during a typical week discussing religious matters or studying religious materials with their children."[6] If parents truly are the greatest spiritual influence on their

---

[6]Barna Research Group, "Parents Accept Responsibility for Their Child's Spiritual Development But Struggle With Effectiveness" May 6, 2003, accessed September 26, 2018, https://www.barna.com/research/parents-accept-responsibility-for-their-childs-spiritual-development-but-struggle-with-effectiveness/.

children as many recent studies have found,[7] the spiritual negligence of parents has surely caused much harm to both the emerging generations and the future of the American Church.

There are many reasons for the spiritual void that is so common at home. Ministry to parents is often complicated by the following challenges: the many stresses faced by single-parent homes, increasingly long work-weeks for parents, which lead to even less family-time, families where one parent is a Christian while the other is not, and the demand upon students' time by school and a host of other extra-curricular activities. Barna's study also found, "Only one out of every five parents of children under 13 has ever been personally contacted or spoken to by a church leader to discuss the parents' involvement in the spiritual life and development of their youngsters."[8] Parents have often been told to do with their children what they are not equipped to do because they have never been discipled themselves. The above-mentioned challenges alongside the absence of a model to follow have conspired against family discipleship in most Christian households.

Youth Culture Reflects a Broader Problem

Youth culture is a direct and unfiltered reflection of the broader culture in which it is located. "Youth culture" arose in the post-industrial revolution where children were removed from factories and given an education in public schools before entering the workplace. Although the concept of "teenager" is relatively new, adolescence has always been recognized and was even mentioned by Aristotle and other ancient figures. It wasn't until the generation following the Industrial Revolution

---

[7]Christian Smith and Melina Lundquist Denton, *Soul Searching: the Religious and Spiritual Lives of American Teenagers* (New York, NY: Oxford University Press, USA, 2005), 56. Vern L. Bengtson, *Families and Faith: How Religion Is Passed Down Across Generations*, (Oxford: Oxford University Press, 2013). Also, Steve Wright and Chris Graves cite multiple non-religious studies affirming the primacy of parental influence in: Steve Wright, *Rethink* (Wake Forest, NC: InQuest Ministries, Inc., 2007), 81-82.
[8]Barna, *Parents Accept Responsibility*.

when adolescence expanded into a socially constructed intermediary stage when the expectations of adulthood were delayed while the child was prepared for future adulthood.[9] As the United States worked to recover from both the Great Depression and the First World War the music, movie, television, radio, and fashion industries began to target the new generation of teenagers. The early generations of adolescents in America found themselves increasingly able to forge their own culture, separate from that of their parents.[10] This period of American history reflects a time where the cultural optimism and increasingly consumerist mindset combined to create youth culture. What was true then is still true today: the overwhelming majority of youth culture is not driven by the youth themselves, but by influential adults who market their products to teenagers. Because youth culture is largely shaped by adults, it should be no surprise that new ideas and trends first show up within youth culture before being introduced to the broader culture—youth have become the proverbial "guinea pigs" of American culture-shapers. Thomas Bergler describes this phenomenon in the American Church as "juvenilization" and defines it this way, "Juvenilization is the process by which the religious beliefs, practices, and developmental characteristics of adolescents become accepted as appropriate for Christians of all ages."[11] While Bergler focuses on how youth culture eventually reshapes the culture-at-large within the church, it is not unreasonable to expect to find similar patterns outside the church.[12]

---

[9]Crystal Kirgiss, *In Search of Adolescence: A New Look at an Old Idea* (San Diego, CA: The Youth Cartel, 2015).

[10]For deeper exploration of this development, see: Andy Root, Faith Formation in a Secular Age (Grand Rapids, MI: Baker Academic, 2017).

[11]Thomas E. Bergler, *The Juvenilization of American Christianity* (Grand Rapids, MI: Eerdmans, 2012), 4.

[12]"Young people pioneered racial integration, created new and exciting methods of evangelism, and gained a newfound sense of their own political power." Bergler, 19-20.

The tragedy of the dropout rate extends far beyond youth ministry, for teenagers provide an unfiltered view of what is happening in the broader religious landscape. In the midst of an increasing number of Americans who are "Religiously Unaffiliated,"[13] it should be no surprise that among the many significant findings of *The National Study on Youth and Religion,* one conclusion was simply, "We'll get what we are."[14] Christian Smith, the lead researcher for the study, wrote, "Any generation gap that exists between teens and adults today is superficial compared with and far outweighed by generational continuity."[15] Despite the years that have passed since Smith's research began, these conclusions continue to be relevant today. Teenagers largely reflect the convictions that have been taught to them by their parents, teachers, and the broader culture.

Smith believes that studying youth culture is particularly helpful because it can serve as a barometer of where broader culture is heading.[16] Youth culture has shown itself to be on the forefront of many sweeping cultural changes. This has been true in the development of music styles, clothing trends, technology, and other matters of faith and morality. Most recently, teenagers have led the way in what is now widespread acceptance of homosexuality. To the culture-watcher, it seems clear that major movements among the emerging generations often spread to the older generations in succeeding order.

In the context of the crisis facing the American Church, the trickle-down effect on youth must be considered. Many of the crises facing youth today originated among adults. At the same time, many proposed solutions for reaching a Postmodern culture of adults were pioneered

---

[13]"'Nones' on the Rise: One-in-Five Adults Have No Religious Affiliation," Pew Research Forum, October 9, 2012, accessed September 26, 2018, http://www.pewforum.org/2012/10/09/nones-on-the-rise/.

[14]Smith, *Soul Searching,* 216.

[15]Smith, *Soul Searching,* 264.

[16]Smith, *Soul Searching,* 6, 191.

in youth ministry. There is an intimate relationship between strategies of youth ministry and the way those strategies are implemented in the broader church when those youth pastors become senior pastors.[17] Lifeway Research and Ligonier Ministries published *The State of Theology* in 2018, which paints a bleak picture of what Americans believe. The following are some of the key statistics, presented to help understand that the religious views of those who are raising teenagers today explains why teenagers are so theologically confused.[18]

- 70% somewhat agree or strongly agree: "There is one true God in three persons: God the Father, God the Son, and God the Holy Spirit."[19]
- 53% somewhat agree or strongly agree: "The Bible has the authority to tell us what we must do."[20]
- 65% somewhat agree or strongly agree: "God accepts the worship of all religions, including Christianity, Judaism, and Islam."[21]
- 57% somewhat agree or strongly agree: "Jesus is the first and greatest being created by God."[22]
- 59% somewhat agree or strongly agree: "The Holy Spirit is a force but is not a personal being."[23]
- 60% somewhat agree or strongly agree: "Religious belief is a matter of personal opinion; it is not about objective truth."[24]

---

[17]For a full exploration of this idea, see: Thomas E. Bergler, *The Juvenilization of American Christianity* (Grand Rapids, MI: Eerdmans, 2012).

[18]Lifeway Research, The *State of American Theology Study 2018*, (Lifeway Research, 2018). Accessed September 26, 2018. PDF available for download, http://lifewayresearch. com/wp-content/uploads/2018/10/Ligonier-State-of-Theology-2018.pdf.

[19]Lifeway Research, *The State of American Theology 2018*, 6.

[20]Ibid, 29.

[21]Ibid, 7.

[22]Ibid, 10.

[23]Ibid, 12.

[24]Ibid, 34.

- 51% somewhat agree or strongly agree: "It is very important for me personally to encourage non-Christians to trust Jesus Christ as their Savior."[25]

Such a glimpse into "adult culture" surely reflects what is increasingly evident among youth. It should serve as no surprise that adults who hold the worldview described above are raising a generation of teenagers who are rejecting Christ and walking away from the Church. This is a crisis facing the entire American Church, for while the first statistic is surprisingly encouraging, some the other statements have been labeled as heretical and distinctly anti-Christian views throughout Christian History.

The younger generations undeniably hold to less biblical views on doctrinal and lifestyle issues than their elders. But they have not come up with these ideas in a vacuum. Recognizing the religious views of parents and other adult influencers on youth culture is vital. In an increasingly transient and post-Christian culture where tolerance is the only universal truth, the Church must begin to discover and capitalize on the many great opportunities to reclaim a prophetic voice into the culture.

Fragmentation Between the Youth Ministry,
the Family, and the Church

Over the last fifty years, youth ministry has emerged as the most significant arm of the church that has ministered to teenagers to ground them in the gospel and equip them for life-long discipleship. Most youth ministers understand their role as one who "comes alongside" parents, and yet this is a great oversight in most youth ministries. The majority of well-respected textbooks used in classrooms to prepare the next generation of youth workers in college or seminary settings have

---

[25]Ibid, 36.

an emphasis on the importance of partnering with parents.[26] Although this is a frequently taught value, it is rarely integrated into the DNA and framework of the youth ministry's programs and teachings because it is so difficult to accomplish. As Wayne Rice has concluded after decades of leadership in youth ministry, "...I've become more and more convinced over the years that God never gave to youth workers the responsibility for making disciples of other people's kids."[27] Similarly, Chap Clark has written, "Youth ministry is not dead, nor is it irrelevant. But it's broken, and we need to do what we can to fix it."[28]

Youth ministry must be seen as the bridge between the local church and the home. When teens are committed more to the youth ministry than to the church, it should be no surprise when many of those teens walk away from their faith after their teen years. In this case, the student's faith commitment was a commitment to that particular Christian community rather than to Christ and the "new people" community known as the church. This is especially challenging for parachurch youth workers who often minister to unchurched students and are unwilling to attend a local church. The importance of intergenerational community and church involvement is hard to over-estimate. Once the youth group community was no longer available, the student's bond with God was shown to be more directed toward the youth group than

---

[26]Doug Fields, *Purpose-Driven Youth Ministry* (Grand Rapids, MI: Zondervan, 1998), 251-268; Doug Fields, *Your First Two Years in Youth Ministry* (El Cajon, CA: Zondervan/Youth Specialties, 2002), 103-125; Wayne Rice, *Reinventing Youth Ministry (again): from Bells and Whistles to Flesh and Blood* (Downers Grove, IL: IVP Books, 2010), 22-35; Marv Penner, *Youth Worker's Guide to Parent Ministry* (Grand Rapids, MI: Zondervan/Youth Specialties, 2003). See also, Mark DeVries, *Family Based Youth Ministry*, Revised and Expanded Edition, (Downers Grove, IL: IVP Books, 2004); Ron Hunter, *The DNA of D6: Building Blocks of Generational Discipleship* (Nashville, TN: Randall House Publications, 2015); Chap Clark, ed. *Adoptive Youth Ministry: Integrating Emerging Generations into the Family of Faith* (Grand Rapids, MI: Baker Academic, 2016).

[27]Rice, *Reinventing Youth Ministry*, 24.

[28]Chap Clark, *Adoptive Church: Creating an Environment Where Emerging Generations Belong* (Grand Rapids, MI: Baker Academic, 2018), 31.

to Christ Himself. This is tragically common and often flows from an incomplete understanding of the gospel. Students are not converted as orphans, but as family members within the Church. Out from this understanding, youth workers patiently disciple unchurched teenagers into embracing their new family identity through participation in the local church.

It is both unhelpful and unwise to consider ministry to the emerging generations to be either the duty of the church or the duty of the family. Instead, churches who are committed to the emerging generations consistently and clearly call parents to disciple their children while providing the resources and partnership necessary to equip the parents to fulfill this great duty. At the same time, the church family comes alongside parents to co-evangelize and co-disciple teenagers through age-targeted ministries. The church and home must not simply encourage each other to fulfill their ministries, they must work in harmony. This approach views youth ministry as a vital component of the church, which serves as a bridge between the home and the church-at-large.

Honest evaluation would find that many church-based youth ministries are functioning as parachurch ministries that are simply sponsored and housed by the local church, but lacking any meaningful partnership. The youth ministry should not be confined to the youth room while being viewed as ministry to kids who are "the church of tomorrow." Instead, the next era of ministry to teenagers needs to pursue a more intimate partnership with the church in order create opportunities for the youth to contribute in meaningful ways to the broader congregation. This philosophy of ministry will greatly affect programming decisions and may lead to decisions that could potentially reduce attendance; but this shift will also lead to a greater long-term impact in students' lives.

Youth ministry is inherently temporary. Teenagers are only "youth" for a few years, and then they become ineligible to continue participation in the ministry. Meanwhile, the church's ministry is ongoing and these young people remain members of a family. Responsible and effective ministry to teenagers must acknowledge the disconnect that often exists between the church, the home, and the youth ministry. If Jonathan Edwards is correct in declaring, "...family education and order are some of the chief means of grace. If these fail, all other means are likely to prove ineffectual. If these are duly maintained, all the means of grace will likely prosper and be successful,"[29] then those who are serving in youth ministry must be intentional and diligent to come alongside parents and equip them to be the primary disciplers of their children. Rather than measuring success by events on the calendar, churches ought to strive for harmony: the church and home singing the same song, in the same key, at the same tempo... together.

"Family Ministry" has become a growing trend in recent years as a recognition of and as a realignment of this disconnect between the church, the youth ministry, and the home. This is a wonderful new emphasis, and yet it seems that although many people are using the same words they are using a different dictionary. This is made clear by Chap Clark's statement that "family ministry emerged without any sort of across-the-board consensus of just what it is. ...Because of this lack of a common perception of family ministry, people responsible for family ministry in churches are often confused and frustrated."[30] It has become abundantly clear that a major shift is taking place throughout youth ministry to correct the tendency to forget the family. Many

---

[29]Jonathan Edwards, ….. as cited in Mark DeVries, *Family-Based Youth Ministry*, 67.

[30]Chap Clark, *The Youth Worker's Handbook to Family Ministry: Strategies and Practical Ideas for Reaching Your Students' Families* (Grand Rapids, MI: Zondervan Publishing Company, 1997), 13; Paul Renfro, Brandon Shields, and Jay Strother, *Perspectives on Family Ministry: 3 Views*, ed. Timothy Paul Jones (Nashville, TN: B&H Academic, 2009), 37-38.

experts in the field of youth ministry are urging a greater intentionality in partnering with parents, and integration within the broader church. Whether youth workers follows the family ministry pathway or the growing "Adoptive Church" model promoted by Chap Clark, which he describes as an effort to help "each and every young person find their place as a faithful follower of Jesus Christ and live as a specifically called agent in the mission of God alongside the family of believers"[31] Regardless of semantics, there is a renewed commitment to seeing the emerging generations grow in Christ through the church and home to partnering together through the youth ministry.

A Fabled Case Study of the "Typical" American Youth Ministry

Mark has been the youth director at his church for four years. He became a Christian as a teenager, so he's passionate about reaching unchurched teenagers with the gospel. The church, however, seems content to have a safe place for teenagers to meet while viewing youth group primarily as a place for fellowship. He tries to remind himself that the church wouldn't pay him a salary or give him a budget if teenagers were as dispensable as he feels they are treated. But as much as he tries, it seems the youth ministry will always be viewed as a ministry that is not well integrated into the life of the church. He desires the students to feel like a meaningful part of the church but has not made any positive traction in making that happen.

Mark understands he's still fairly young, and he's the first to admit he probably is not the best person to disciple the parents of teens. The commitments students break make it painfully clear that sports and school are more important than anything going on at church. Students arrive late or leave early from retreats due to sports. They are

---

[31]Chap Clark, *Adoptive Church*, 19.

absent from important leadership team or missions team preparation meetings because of work other commitments that could have been rescheduled. Mark is more frustrated with the parents than he is with the students because they allow this to happen while treating him like he needs to lighten up. He stews over the question, "How can they not see they are setting their kids up to love grades and success more than Jesus? They're training their kids to put their faith in the backseat!" He is convinced that students are so busy it is unhealthy, even potentially dangerous; but when he expresses this concern to parents they disagree. The parents are not concerned about their teens' busyness, they are happy about it because it "Keeps them out of trouble."

In a conversation with Mark you hear him talk about the important role parents have in their children's spiritual development, and yet there are obvious undertones of tension between him and the parents. Mark believes parents should take greater initiative in their kids' spiritual growth, but he is not hopeful that will actually happen. And yet, despite the rather distant relationship, parents believe Mark is doing a good job.

Most of the parents in Mark's ministry are either unengaged or they help in simple ways like providing snacks and driving for special events. Even as Mark desires to see parents meaningfully invest in the youth ministry, he's hesitant to trust them with significant responsibilities because he's been burned in the past. The most consistent input he has received from parents has been to view youth group as a place for Christian students to have fellowship. Few parents seem to view the youth ministry as a place for the Great Commission and significant discipleship to take place.

He has faithfully labored for these last four years and has emphasized evangelism to unchurched students. Mark leads youth group with a team of volunteers who love Jesus and are committed to reaching the next generation with the gospel. They do a good job setting an atmosphere where students are welcomed and feel loved. There are a few key students who seem to be growing in their faith and are trying to minister to their peers, but Mark struggles with discouragement about the spiritual apathy many students demonstrate. His two primary goals for the next three years are to get more families involved in the ministry and to raise up a team of student leaders, but he is not entirely confident he will succeed in reaching those goals. And on his drive home from youth group, he often wonders if it is time to rethink his overall youth ministry strategy.

Mark's story above is based off interviews with over 2000 parents and youth workers, as reported in a collaborative study by Youth Specialties, YouthWorks, and the Barna Group and published in, *The State of Youth Ministry*.[32] This is further corroborated in a self-initiated poll conducted with 273 youth workers, most of whom are paid for full-time or part-time ministry where the majority of youth pastors confess parents are minimally involved in the ministry and name evangelism as their ministry's greatest weaknesses. Yet, most say they would change either nothing or only a few things to tweak their ministry. If the above narratives are as common as it seems, something needs to change. The problem is not a lack of biblical passion on behalf of youth workers. Instead, the very foundations of the church's ministry to teenagers needs to be reevaluated and firmly established on what the Bible teaches.

Studies repeatedly bear witness to the transforming nature of adolescence. Why, then, would anyone approach youth ministry differently than they would approach "real" ministry? Teenagers need the same gospel, the same commitment to discipleship, the same type of training for evangelism and ministry, and the same warning that God refines faith through suffering (rather than promising to be rescued from it).

---

[32]The Barna Group, *The State of Youth Ministry: How Churches Reach Today's Teens—and What Parents Think About It* (Barna Group, 2016).

Chapter 2

The Old Testament and Youth Ministry

The desire for generational faithfulness is as old as faith itself. Looking to Scripture seems to be an afterthought in the discussions and debates regarding the "dropout rate," as if the Bible is silent about raising a faithful generation. This was a central component of Jewish identity and the Old Testament abounds with examples of Israel's commitment to their young. There is no verse that explicitly commands youth ministry, but the family and the community's mandate to raise up the next generation in the fear and obedience of the LORD is overwhelming. Biblical youth ministry is a modern application of the frequent commands to pass on the commands of God to the next generation. The Bible, and especially the Old Testament, emphasizes that parents are given the primary responsibility of evangelizing and discipling their children.

The temple did not employ youth workers who organized games, service projects, and Bible lessons; but the broader community played a vital role in ministry to the next generation. Parents were given the primary calling to impress the commands of Scripture on their children's minds and hearts, but this was never meant for parents alone. Because parents would be raising their children on the family compound, surrounded by extended family and the broader community, all the generations of Israel were expected to come together in order to raise up the younger generations for covenantal faithfulness.

Accordingly, this chapter will focus on the Old Testament's command to Israel regarding the family discipleship (Deuteronomy 6:4-9), a powerful and enduring warning regarding the failure to minister to the next generation (Joshua 24; Judges 2:10), and examples of both intergenerational worship (Psalm 71:18; 78) and an example of the separation of children in worship (Nehemiah 8:1-3).

Deuteronomy 6:4-9

> *"Hear, O Israel: The LORD our God, the LORD is one.*
> *You shall love the LORD your God with all your heart and with*
> *all your soul and with all your might. And these words that I*
> *command you today shall be on your heart. You shall teach them*
> *diligently to your children, and shall talk of them when you sit in your*
> *house, and when you walk by the way, and when you lie down, and*
> *when you rise. You shall bind them as a sign on your hand, and they*
> *shall be as frontlets between your eyes. You shall write them on the door-*
> *posts of your house and on your gates."*
> (Deuteronomy 6:4–9) [33]

Historical context is imperative to understanding this passage's significance for Israel. At this point in Israel's history, they had been freed from slavery in Egypt, walked through the Red Sea, witnessed the LORD delivering the Law to Moses on Mt. Sinai, and wandered in the desert for decades. All this took place under the leadership of Moses, who knew his death was coming soon. In Deuteronomy, Moses himself is serving as the shepherd to a generation who grew up under his leadership and he is calling them to renew the covenant their parents

---

[33]Note, all Bible translations are taken from the ESV unless otherwise noted. English Standard Version, (Wheaton, IL: Crossway, 2010).

had made with the LORD. His intention was to clearly communicate the foundational identity of Israel to the next generation: God's chosen people.

> *"Hear, O Israel: The LORD our God, the LORD is one.*
> *Love the LORD your God with all your heart and*
> *with all your soul and with all your strength."*
> (Deuteronomy 6:4-5)

The importance of this text begins with the imperative שְׁמַע *(šᵉma),* "Hear!" This is a call for attention, gathering Israel's together and giving an obvious clue that what is coming next is of utmost importance. Not only does שְׁמַע serve as a call to listen, its form also carries the implied meaning that "to hear God without putting into effect the command is not to hear Him at all."[34] שְׁמַע is akin to starting a sermon by saying, "Listen up, this is really important!"

Yahweh is referred to as "our God," explicitly linking both the former and the current generation's identity as the people of God.[35] God's promises to their parents were also His promises to them: they are God's chosen people. It must be remembered that although monotheism is the majority view in the American context, it was radically divergent and strange in Ancient Near Eastern culture. Monotheism distinguished Israel from all the other peoples of their time. The LORD, *Elohim,* made Abraham the father of a great nation, Israel, and He later revealed Himself to Moses and Israel as their covenant God, Yahweh (Genesis 12:1-3; Exodus 3:14.). The temptation for Israel to forsake the Law, especially the second commandment prohibiting idolatry, was a very real temptation, and Moses wanted to command Israel as clearly and forcefully as possible to remember their identity fully relied on the

---

[34]Eugene H. Merrill, *Deuteronomy,* vol. 4, *The New American Commentary* (Nashville, TN: B&H Publishing Group, 1994), 162.
[35]Translated in English Bible translations as LORD, with all capital letters.

LORD. This is why Deuteronomy 6:4, commonly known as the *Shema*, is the first verse Jewish children have been taught for millennia. This set Israel apart from all other nations, that Yahweh is one God and that Israel must only worship Him.

Israel's identity was intimately connected to the LORD, mediated through the Abrahamic, Mosaic, and Davidic Covenants. Israel's covenant obedience was to be fueled by faithful love, not obligatory duty or cold-hearted ceremony (Amos 5:1; Hosea 6:6). Eugene Merrill explains that God, "demands of them unqualified obedience. The depth and breadth of that expectation is elaborated upon by the fact that it encompasses the heart, soul, and strength of God's people...."[36] According to the Ancient Near Eastern mindset, the heart was the seat of the intellect, the soul referred to the intangible characteristics such as the will and desires, while strength clearly pointed one's attention to physical abilities.[37] Peter Craigie places this commandment as the central verse of the entire book of Deuteronomy, with the remainder as a description of how Israel is meant to fulfill the command to love God with all their heart, soul, and strength.[38]

Christians interpret the Old Covenant in light of the New. Therefore, no Christian should overlook Jesus' teaching that Deuteronomy 6:5 is the "first and greatest commandment."[39] Because the gospel brings a new identity as a child of God, Christians are called to live differently than the world (John 1:12; Romans 12:1-2). God's people ought to be marked by love: love for God that is so life-transforming others are loved more than oneself. In the same way that Israel em-

---

[36]Merrill, *Deuteronomy*, 164.
[37]Merrill, *Deuteronomy*, 164.
[38]Peter C. Craigie, *The Book of Deuteronomy*, 2nd ed., *The New International Commentary on the Old Testament* (Grand Rapids, MI: Eerdmans, 1976),169.
[39]Matt. 22:36-38; Mark 12:28-31; Luke 10:25-28. Merrill provides a thorough and compelling analysis of the use of Deut. 6:5 in the Synoptic Gospels cited above: see, Merrill, *Deuteronomy*, 164-6.

braced the Shema as their identity-marker, Christians live according to the gospel of grace. Christian identity drives the Christian's lifestyle because he has been adopted as a son or daughter of God. Deuteronomy 6:4-5 reminds the people of God to remember their identity before they develop their rituals, lest the faithful forget their obedience flows from their identity rather than the other way around.

> *"These commandments that I give you today are to be on your hearts. Impress them on your children. Talk about them when you sit at home and when you walk along the road, when you lie down and when you get up. Tie them as symbols on your hands and bind them on your foreheads. Write them on the doorframes of your houses and on your gates."*
>
> Deuteronomy 6:6-9 (NIV)

Now that Moses has reminded Israel who they are and instructed them what they ought to do, he directs them regarding how to accomplish it. "These commandments" refer back to the entire covenant they have recommitted themselves to, especially Deuteronomy 6:4-5.[40] One must remember that in this context "heart" does not refer to the emotions, as it does today, but to the intellect, as already mentioned above.

Duane Christensen makes the connection between the close of verse 6, "These commandments...are to be on your hearts," and the promise in Jeremiah 31:31-33, where Yahweh says He will make a new covenant with Israel whereby "I will put my law within them, and I will write it on their hearts."[41] This connection reminds the Christian, the Law was never able to save anyone, because no one has been able to keep it perfectly. Instead, the Law was given to God's people to remind

---

[40]Merrill, *Deuteronomy*, 167.

[41]Duane L. Christensen, *Deuteronomy 1:1-21:9*, vol. 6, 2nd ed., *Word Biblical Commentary* (Grand Rapids, MI: Thomas Nelson, 2001), 143.

them of the basis of their salvation: the gracious provision of God. As Paul wrote in Romans 7:22-25,

> For I delight in the law of God, in my inner being, but I see in my members another law waging war against the law of my mind and making me captive to the law of sin that dwells in my members. Wretched man that I am! Who will deliver me from this body of death? Thanks be to God through Jesus Christ our Lord! So then, I myself serve the law of God with my mind, but with my flesh I serve the law of sin.

Those who use Deuteronomy 6 as the foundation for family discipleship often overlook this vital reminder and fall into a pattern of prescribing God's commandments to children as if they will be able to keep the Law if they are taught at an early enough age.

In the Hebrew language, the Piel verb form is an intensifier that makes a basic word (like "hit") into a stronger word (like "smash"). Moses wrote verses 7-9 in this way to emphasize to Israel the significance of this command regarding the instruction of their children. The intensity of the instruction in verse 7 to *"Impress them on your children"* is translated as "impress," וְשִׁנַּנְתָּם *(wᵉšinnantām)*, and carries the clear image of a craftsman engraving an image. Likewise, parents are to carefully, skillfully, and diligently impress God's commandments into their children's hearts. Because the commandments are not constrained to Temple-worship but involve every aspect of Israel's life, the manner of this instruction is to take place continually, regardless of location or time.

This does not require parents to deliver a daily sermon or lecture; instead, they are conversational and explanatory in nature, clarifying why Israel is unique among other nations. Moses is using hyperbole regarding the frequency of instruction, though he certainly is communicating that these discussions must happen, and they must happen frequently from parent to child.[42] There should be both intentional, structured time (impress them on your children's heart) and casual teaching that arises throughout the day (talk of them when you sit in your house and when you walk by the way, when you lie down and when you rise).

The call to bind the commandments of the LORD on one's hands and forehead and doorposts in verses 8-9 again reflects the Piel intensifier and is symbolic, and yet there are many who took these instructions literally. Phylacteries and mezuzah, boxes containing portions of the Torah, were worn on foreheads and posted on doorframes, respectively. Rather than being a literal command, this ought to serve as a reminder that every thought (head), every deed (hand), and every home (doorpost) must reflect the love of God, which is commanded in verses 4-5. When parents' love for God is at the center of everything they do, their children will not only be instructed in the faith but also given a model to follow. On the other hand, when the commands of God are rarely seen in the life of parents, children may hear them taught but are learning them as abstract principles that are not lived out in the real world.

James Hamilton interprets the second person singular form of "you" in verses 7-9 to mean, "as Moses addressed that nation of Israel, he directed the responsibility to teach the 'sons' toward the fathers. ... Moses did not give this responsibility to some abstract group of fathers in the community but to each individual father. It doesn't take a village; it takes a father."[43] While he is correct regarding the verb forms, none of the major commentaries on Deuteronomy draw the same conclusion. If the command is meant to be entirely literal, then Moses' address in

---

[42]Merrill, *Deuteronomy*, 167.

[43]James M. Hamilton, Jr., "That the Coming Generation Might Praise the Lord: Family Discipleship in the Old Testament," in *Trained in the Fear of God: Family Ministry in Theological, Historical, and Practical Perspective*, ed. Randy Stinson & Timothy Paul Jones (Grand Rapids, MI: Kregel Academic & Professional, 2011), 37.

the singular should mean he was only instructing one father. The male gender of these verbs may reflect the priority of the father's responsibility to lead in this instruction, but it may also simply reflect that gender would default to the male grammatical forms in mixed company. If we allow for a more symbolic sense where Moses is addressing a group of people (*"Hear, O Israel"*), it seems inconsistent to understand his instruction being *only* for fathers. The responsibility for the instruction of children is primarily on their parents, but within the broader context of Israel's corporate identity and calling.

It is important to remember that Israel's conception of the family was broader than the nuclear family. The Jewish family typically lived in a family compound as one clan. The generations lived together, and the idea of parents moving to another village with their children was strange and uncommon. This is one aspect of Abraham's call in Genesis 12 that was so unique and challenging: families stayed together. This seems to indicate a strong communal setting for the commands to follow. While it is right for the father to lead in family discipleship, it is also biblical for his wife to be his "helper" as Eve helped Adam fulfill his duty before God.[44]

Deuteronomy 6:4-9 is the foundational passage on family discipleship because it is so clear and instructive on the parents' duty to their children. While parents are primarily responsible to raise their children to love the LORD their God, these commands are for parents within the context of Israel as a whole. The generations of Israel are together commanded to pass on the faith to their children, and they are judged as a people for their failure to do so.

---

[44]See Chapter 6 for more on this.

Joshua 24:14-15 & Judges 2:7-10

> *"Now therefore fear the Lord and serve him in sincerity and in faithfulness. Put away the gods that your fathers served beyond the River and in Egypt, and serve the Lord. And if it is evil in your eyes to serve the Lord, choose this day whom you will serve, whether the gods your fathers served in the region beyond the River, or the gods of the Amorites in whose land you dwell. But as for me and my house, we will serve the Lord."*
> (Joshua 24:14–15)

The similarities between Deuteronomy 6 and Joshua 24 run deep. Both give the account of a covenant renewal between Israel and the Lord, which is led by a great leader of Israel shortly before his death. In the opening portion of Joshua 24, he recounts to Israel the covenant faithfulness of the Lord: from Abraham, Isaac, and Jacob, to their miraculous deliverance out of Egypt, and most recently their victory over the inhabitants of the Promised Land. Joshua reminds Israel that everything they have has come from the hand of God. Now, in verse 14, he urges them to fear the Lord and serve him by putting away their idolatry and walking in faithful service to the Lord.

The *"fear of the Lord"* is a regular theme in the Old Testament and is marked by three attributes: holy reverence, humble confession, and obedient faith. As the believer discovers the holiness of God, he is drawn into a fearful sense of God's grandeur and sovereignty. The attempt to control or manipulate God melts into humble confession of sin and leads into an acknowledgement of unworthiness to receive anything other than God's judgment. When sin is confessed and God is worshiped as holy and gracious, the natural overflow is one of obedience to the Word of the Lord. Joshua commands Israel to fear the Lord and to serve Him with sincerity and faithfulness.

While Deuteronomy 6 does not explicitly mention "*the fear of the Lord,*" the overlapping call to "love the Lord your God with all your heart, soul, mind, and strength" should be seen as complementary calls to covenant faithfulness. Israel's conquest is now behind them and as the Lord's promises to the Patriarchs are fulfilled, they are given one final warning to "put away" the gods of the nations and to choose whether or not they will fully embrace their identity as the people of God.

> "*And the people served the Lord all the days of Joshua, and all the days of the elders who outlived Joshua, who had seen all the great work that the Lord had done for Israel. And Joshua the son of Nun, the servant of the Lord, died at the age of 110 years. And they buried him within the boundaries of his inheritance in Timnath-heres, in the hill country of Ephraim, north of the mountain of Gaash. And all that generation also were gathered to their fathers. And there arose another generation after them who did not know the Lord or the work that he had done for Israel.*"
>
> (Judges 2:7–10)

Moses stressed the importance for Israel to raise their children in the love of the Lord and to teach them faithfulness to God's commandments. Joshua's generation, however, focused only on adult discipleship and was silent regarding the next generation. The people of Israel lived faithfully under the rule of Joshua, but their children did not fear the Lord or serve Him. This is given in Scripture as a severe warning for future generations.

It is unclear how many generations passed between Joshua's generation and those who "*did not know the Lord or the work that he had done for Israel.*" It is implied that the elders feared the Lord and the generation who immediately followed did not. An important clarification is helpful: by saying they did not know the Lord or what He had done for Israel, the writer is not implying they had no knowledge about the Lord or Israel's history. Instead, the Hebrew text says Israel לֹא־יָדְעוּ (lō '-yāḏeʿû), "they did not know." This verb can simply be translated as "to know," but it always carries the implication of intimate knowledge. This may be the same kind of "knowing" that Adam had for Eve before they conceived children. Likewise, in Proverbs 3:6 it translated as, "In all your ways *acknowledge him,* and he will make straight your paths." This exegetical background is helpful to clarify that this faithless generation may have known the factual information about the Lord and about the Exodus, but they did not know God in the intimate and personal sense. They did not love Him (Deuteronomy 6:5) or fear Him (Joshua 24:14). Instead, they followed the Baals and served them (Judges 2:11-13).

The idolatry and faithlessness of this generation in Judges 2:10 is significant. God's promises to Abraham to become a great nation was fulfilled through the twelve tribes who received their allotments in Israel (Joshua 13—21), and only one generation later the Promised Land is filled with Baal worship. As the Lord kept His promise to Abraham, so He kept His warning to Israel about the judgment that would fall upon them if they forsook Him. Judges 2:14-15 records, "*So the anger of the Lord was kindled against Israel, and he gave them over to plunderers, who plundered them. And he sold them into the hand of their surrounding enemies, so that they could no longer withstand their enemies. Whenever they marched out, the hand of the Lord was against them for harm, as the Lord had warned, and as the Lord had sworn to them. And they were in terrible distress.*" It was a mighty and wonderful thing for Israel to receive the fulfillment of Abraham's promise, but the bliss was short-lived due to their failure to pass on their faith to the next generation. Beginning with this generation, the remainder of Israel's history is an ongoing cycle of warning, repentance, and idolatry.

Israel's failure to evangelize and disciple the next generation led to their own downfall. This intergenerational mission may not seem like the most pressing need for adults who have many other burdens, however, Joshua's generation is presented as a horrific warning to Israel.

Psalms 71:17 & 78:1-8

The Psalmist continues with Israel's call to raise the next generation to remember the LORD and to serve Him. This should be no surprise, since the Psalms are the hymnal of the Old Testament. The Psalms reflect Israel's commitment to learn from the warning of Joshua's generation and provide an experiential way for the younger generations to hear and cherish the mighty works of God. These emphases are most clearly reflected in Psalm 71:17 and throughout Psalm 78.

> *"So even to old age and gray hairs, O God,*
> *do not forsake me, until I proclaim your might to*
> *another generation, your power to all those to come."*
> (Psalms 71:18)

God's faithfulness has been emphasized throughout Psalm 71, and now the Psalmist's motivation rises in verse 18. His desire is to recount the powerful works of the LORD so the younger generation would remain faithful. Rather than giving in to old age as an invitation to withdraw from the younger generations, the psalmist leans in toward the young so they would remember the works of the LORD.

As the Psalms were repeated in Israel's worship, this approach to the next generation was a regular affirmation of the priority Israel placed on the older discipling the younger. Discipleship was not a duty for parents alone, but was integrated into the communal worship of Israel. The faithful elders of the Jewish community made it a priority to ensure the children were raised according to the knowledge of God's mighty works for Israel. This was not the sole duty of parents, it was shared between parents and the community of faith. Parents are consistently affirmed as the primary disciple-makers of their children, but the

Psalmist's example clearly shows the commitment of the community toward the young.

> *"Give ear, O my people, to my teaching; incline your ears to the words of my mouth! I will open my mouth in a parable; I will utter dark sayings from of old, things that we have heard and known, that our fathers have told us. We will not hide them from their children, but tell to the coming generation the glorious deeds of the Lord, and his might, and the wonders that he has done. He established a testimony in Jacob and appointed a law in Israel, which he commanded our fathers to teach to their children, that the next generation might know them, the children yet unborn, and arise and tell them to their children, so that they should set their hope in God and not forget the works of God, but keep his commandments; and that they should not be like their fathers, a stubborn and rebellious generation, a generation whose heart was not steadfast, whose spirit was not faithful to God."*
>
> (Psalms 78:1–8)

Psalm 78:1-8 serves as a preamble for the remainder of this long psalm of praise that recounts God's saving work and provision for Israel. The Psalm is crafted in a way that could be easily sung and taught to the young. This is a clear attempt to fulfill Moses' instruction in Deuteronomy 6:4-9, while avoiding the example set by the generation after Joshua. The liturgy of the Psalms was a multi-generational effort, crafted to reflect the community's calling to the youth. This cannot be stressed enough—the liturgy of Jewish worship was developed with a leading emphasis on ministry to children. This Psalm was written as a warning to the Southern Kingdom (Israel) after the fall of the Northern Kingdom (Ephraim). Verses 9-11 clearly points to this event by stating, *"The Ephraimites, armed with the bow, turned back on the day of battle. They did not keep God's covenant, but refused to walk according to his law. They forgot his works and the wonders that he had shown them."* They had seen with their own eyes that God will judge His people for their faithlessness. Because the commandments of the LORD were not kept, and because the children of Ephraim did not remember the LORD they received the judgment promised in Deuteronomy 6:14-15.

Moses' generation was faithful to pass the faith from one generation to the next; but Joshua's generation did not, and neither did it continue in Ephraim. The LORD was faithful to the promises He made to Israel: He established Israel in the faithful generations, and He disciplined those who were unfaithful. Finally, the LORD withdrew His patience and delivered the promised judgment when the Northern Kingdom (Ephraim) fell to the Assyrians (2 Kings 17:3-6). Psalm 78 subtly issues the same challenge as Joshua, "Choose this day whom you will serve." Now that the Southern Kingdom is all that remains in the Promised Land, they must decide whether they will be faithful to their covenant with the LORD.

Whereas printed Bibles are commonly available today, Israel relied on memory as they heard the Word of God read and declared. This explains a key reason why the Psalms are so important: they demonstrate how children and adults were instructed in the faith. Derek Kidner explains regarding Psalm 78, "Like the parting song of Moses (Deuteronomy 32) it is meant to search the conscience: it is history that must not repeat itself. At the same time, it is meant to warm the heart, for it tells of great miracles, of a grace that persists through all the judgments, and of the promise that displays its tokens in the chosen city and chosen king."[45] This is a beautiful example of the power of the Psalms in the spiritual life of Israel.

It is noteworthy that the young were taught. They were instructed to "incline their ears" and to receive instruction. And yet, the mature in the congregation did not simply lecture, but taught about the LORD's

---

[45]Derek Kidner, *Psalms 73–150: A Commentary on Books III-V of the Psalms,* Tyndale Old Testament Commentaries, vol. 16 (Downers Grove, IL: InterVarsity Press, 1975), 280.

covenantal faithfulness through singing. The aim of this instruction was not mere compliance, but that the next generation would *"set their hope in God and not forget the works of God"* (v.7). What a wonderful prayer for the next generation! The Psalmist is reminding Israel what the LORD has done and is commanding them to tell their children. It is his attempt to lead Israel into covenant faithfulness and to warn of the judgment that will come if they are faithless. In this way, Psalm 78 is an example of Israel's attempt to heed the command given in Deuteronomy 6 while remembering the example of the generation after Joshua.

Nehemiah 8:1-2

> *"And all the people gathered as one man into the square before the Water Gate. And they told Ezra the scribe to bring the Book of the Law of Moses that the LORD had commanded Israel. So Ezra the priest brought the Law before the assembly, both men and women and all who could understand what they heard, on the first day of the seventh month. And he read from it facing the square before the Water Gate from early morning until midday, in the presence of the men and the women and those who could understand. And the ears of all the people were attentive to the Book of the Law."*
> (Nehemiah 8:1–3)

This was a momentous day when all the people gathered, men and women, rich and poor, so long as they were able to understand. Upon rebuilding the walls of Jerusalem after the Exile, Ezra gathered the people of Israel to reaffirm their covenant with the LORD. This was an unusually large gathering of all Israel, so much that a special platform was constructed for the occasion. And yet Nehemiah 8:2 clearly says, *"all who could understand what they heard"* were invited. This short phrase is overlooked by nearly every commentator, but is noteworthy.

Infants and young children were absent from this gathering, and they surely were not left home unattended. It is possible that the exclusion of children was the result of the people's waywardness and indicated spiritual neglect of the youngest Israelites, although the text gives no indication that Israel did anything wrong by only inviting those who were old enough to understand. Instead, Nehemiah seems to be writing in a way that celebrates Israel's act of faithfulness without any hint of criticism for the infants and young children being present. Given the significance of the moment, it is natural to conclude that attendance would have been broader, rather than more restricted, than a typical gathering. Because children were excused from this situation it is likely they would have been excused from a normal gathering. Israel's corporate identity embraced a default toward the generations being together, yet this instance shows there were times when children were not in the assembly.

A further question may be asked regarding what it means to "understand" and at what age is a child considered mature. Those who answer with a tighter answer might indicate that only infants and the youngest children were excluded; while a broader answer could stretch until children have completed their education in the Jewish Law, which was usually around twelve years old. Of the commentaries who mention the children in Nehemiah 8:2, most seem to agree with Adam Clarke's explanation, "Infants, idiots, and children not likely to receive instruction, were not permitted to attend this meeting."[46] The phrase "all who understand" (כָּל מֵבִין) is also found in 2 Chronicles 34:12 in reference to *"all who were skillful with instruments of music."* Additional study on the Old Testament's use of the Hiphil בִּין ("understand") reveals a tendency toward the broader meaning. Proverbs 28:7, Isaiah 1:3, Isaiah 29:16, 1 Kings 3:11 and other similar passages all use the Hiphil to

---

[46]Adam Clarke, *Adam Clarke's Commentary on the Whole Bible,* (Altamonte Springs, FL: OakTree Software, 2004), paragraph 13274.

communicate understanding, comprehension, and wisdom. So it is quite possible to view "all who understand" in 8:2 as those who have the knowledge and maturity to receive the book of the Law of Moses and obey it. Nehemiah 8:8 also seems to support a broader view where the people respond in a way that demonstrated they "understood (בִין) the reading."

The precise age range of those who were not present remains unclear, debatable, and largely unaddressed by the majority of major commentaries. This is perhaps the clearest example in the Old Testament regarding age-targeted ministry within the covenant community. At the very least, this verse provides a clear biblical precedent for having offering nursery care for infants and young children during worship services. Meanwhile the broader interpretation of "those who understand" opens a variety of children's ministries, while the aim remains integration within the faith community. Regardless, this does reveal that even in the midst of Israel's commitment to intergenerational unity, there were times when the children were separated. Caution must be taken by those who would rush towards building a framework for age-targeted ministry on this one verse—thankfully, this is not the only verse in the Bible that provides guidance and examples of ministry to children and youth.

Conclusion: Ministry to the Next Generation in the Old Testament

Raising the next generation in the fear of the LORD was of utmost importance to Israel. Without this generational faithfulness, all Israel would surely break the covenant and fall under judgment. Therefore, children were instructed from a young age regarding their identity and corresponding expectations as covenant children. Parents were the primary teachers of their children, both through formal teaching and by setting a faithful example; and yet parents lived in a broader family and community context than modern families experience. The Psalms demonstrate that children were frequently in mind during the corporate gathering of God's people. At the same time, Nehemiah 8:1-3 is an example where the Old Testament simultaneously describes a gathering of "all the people" even while "all who could not understand what they heard" were excused from the assembly.

Without a doubt, parents are entrusted as disciple-makers of the next generation. Even while stressing the importance of family discipleship, non-parental adults and the broader faith-community provide a formative influence in the lives of children and adolescents. The generation after Joshua serves as a reminder that making disciples of the next generation must be a regular priority among the people of God, not only for the parents and the children/youth ministry leaders. A commitment to children and adolescents should be reflected not only through families but also through the community's gathered time for worship. At the same time, Nehemiah 8:1-3 demonstrates that even while the default should be intergenerational togetherness, there is a measure of freedom for churches to determine the best way to care for and instruct the children while the adults also receive instruction.

Chapter 3

The New Testament and Youth Ministry

In the quest to discern the Bible's guidance for ministry to the next generation, many books understandably focus on the Old Testament, primarily on Deuteronomy 6. While this is obviously a good and healthy place to begin, the New Testament has much to offer beyond Jesus' statement *"let the little children come to me"* (Matthew 19:14). Comprehending the world in which Jesus and the apostles lived opens a window to help us see not only *what* they taught but *how* they conducted their ministries. There are only a few, brief explicit references to intergenerational discipleship in the New Testament, but there are portraits of it painted throughout. This chapter explores the ministry culture of Jesus and the apostles' contemporaries while also considering those particular verses that mention the older generation's ministry to the younger.

Jesus and the Apostles

Jesus was not the first teacher to take disciples. It was a common practice that respected teachers would receive students who would follow him in order to become like their master, both in life and in wisdom. The Greek word, μαθητής (*mathétés*), conveys multiple layers of discipleship. In a sense it simply means "a follower," because the disciple wanders from place to place with and learns how to imitate the life of his master. Another sense is that of "a student" who is being taught and trained in the way of knowledge, wisdom, and skill. In this way, the biblical portrait of a disciple is deeply personal and intimate. Jesus' ministry to the apostles, disciples, and the crowds did not originate in a vacuum. Instead, there are various contemporary patterns of discipleship that influenced the way the Bible views discipleship.

Biblical Precursors of Discipleship From the Greek World

Discipleship was not created by Jesus or the early Christians. There are examples of Disciple-Master relationships throughout the ancient world. Rengstorf explains in the landmark *Theological Dictionary of the New Testament,* "The almost technical sense of the word, which implies a direct dependence of the one under instruction upon an authority superior in knowledge, and which emphasizes the fact that this relation cannot be dissolved, controls the whole usage...."[47] To be a disciple was to enter into a personal relationship with a master where more than facts and information were being conveyed; a disciple was trained to not only learn from his master, but to become like him.

In Michael J. Wilkins' excellent book, *Following the Master: A Biblical Theology of Discipleship,* he explores the Greek foundations for discipleship. He explains, "From its very earliest use, *mathétés* was not simply a learner or a pupil in an academic setting. In fact, Herodotus, in whose writings the noun occurs for the first time in written Greek, uses the term to indicate a person who made a significant, personal, life commitment."[48] Discipleship has never been a purely intellectual exercise; it has always been intensely personal.

---

[47]K.H. Rengstorf, "μαθητής" in Kittel, Gerhard, G. W. Bromiley, and Gerhard Friedrich *Theological Dictionary of the New Testament,* vol. 4 (Grand Rapids, MI: Eerdmans, 1967), 416.

[48]Michael J. Wilkins, *Following the Master: A Biblical Theology of Discipleship* (Grand Rapids, MI: Zondervan, 1992), 75.

A disciple's credibility was inextricably linked to his master. Perhaps the most well-known non-biblical example is that of Socrates and Plato. Considering that Socrates was put to death in 399 BC for "corrupting the youth," it only makes sense to conclude that his primary audience were youths, not adults. Socrates' emphasis on educating the younger generations is reflected through Plato and the broader Socratic-legacy. Everything credited to Socrates has been preserved and transmitted through the writings of Plato, Euclid, and others disciples who passed his teachings down through their own writings. Through their commitment not only to his ideas, but also to his character, Socrates has continued to inspire future philosophers. And yet, when he is quoted or referenced, it is not Socrates but, in fact, Plato or another disciple who recorded their master's teachings.

Rabbinic Patterns of Discipleship

As the previous chapter emphasized, Israel placed great emphasis on passing the faith from one generation to the next. This commitment is recorded in the Mishna, a collection of oral tradition that was taught by the Rabbis, but only written down in the early Third Century. The teachings of the Mishna reflect common Jewish practices and teachings that were taught and passed from generation to generation, especially in the First and Second Century. The Mishna commends the following timeline for study of the Torah:

(1) At five to Scripture, (2) ten to Mishnah, (3) thirteen to religious duties, (4) fifteen to Talmud, (5) eighteen to the wedding canopy, (6) twenty to responsibility for providing for a family, (7) thirty to fullness of strength, (8) forty to understanding, (9) fifty to counsel, (10) sixty to old age, (11) seventy to ripe old age, (12) eighty to remarkable strength, (13) ninety to a

bowed back, and (14) at a hundred—he is like a corpse who has already passed and gone from this world.[49]

In the Jewish world, Rabbinic Tradition is built around the passing on of wisdom and insight surrounding the Law of Moses and how to live in accordance with it. These teachings were taught through oral tradition from one generation to the next and from rabbi to disciple. Not all students, however, would continue in their training to become rabbis or teachers themselves. For instance, the school of Shammai was more difficult to enter than the school of Hillel, although all rabbis were known to reject unworthy students.[50] To study under a rabbi was a highly sought after honor; such that it may have been considered as a higher priority than the commandment to honor one's parents. Keritot 6:9 records, "If the son acquired merit [by sitting and studying] before the master, the master takes precedence over the father under all circumstances." Peah 1:1 provides a list of matters in life of the utmost priority, including honoring one's father and mother, and then concludes, "But the study of Torah is as important as all of them together." This teaching of the Mishna is likely the root cause of Jesus' rebuke of the Pharisees in Matthew 15:1-9, because some Pharisees were putting this into practice in a way that overrode the commands of God.

Rabbis typically did not accept payment for their teaching, though it was commonly encouraged for the faithful to show hospitality to itinerant rabbis and their disciples. The itinerant rabbi would move from town to town, sometimes for only a few days and other times for weeks, and would teach to whatever sized crowd would come hear him. While the crowds enjoyed the rabbis public teachings, the disciples were encouraged to ask questions, for "a shy person [will not] learn" (Avot 2:5). Disciples would often be given more detailed explanations and

---

[49]Avot 5:21.
[50]Reinhard Neudecker, "Master-Disciple / Disciple-Master Relationship in Rabbinic Judaism and in the Gospels," *Gregorianum* 80:2 (1999), 249.

interpretations in private, such as Jesus' explanation of the Parable of the Sower to His disciples in Matthew 13:16-23. Not only did a rabbi's disciples make the necessary sacrifice to follow him for these private interpretations, "he learned in a very practical way how the master translated religious law into daily practice."[51] The rabbi's life became a living sermon.

Jesus as Rabbi

Jesus followed certain aspects of contemporary rabbinic practices, however, Andreas Köstenberger notes two primary differences between Jesus as rabbi and the other rabbis of His day.[52] First, Jesus relied on His own spiritual authority rather than on rabbinic training. This is most clearly demonstrated in the Sermon on the Mount where Jesus repeatedly says, "You have heard it said...but I say to you." This is unexpected because rabbis saw their authority as a borrowed-authority—dependent upon the Scriptures and the oral tradition in which they were trained. The second difference highlights the unique origin of Jesus' relationship with His disciples. Jesus chose His disciples rather than the other way around. While it was common rabbinic practice for the rabbi to choose whether or not to accept someone as a disciple, the rabbi himself very rarely gave the personal invitation for someone to become a disciple. Reflecting these same two differences, Craig Blomberg writes, "Jesus' behavior stood typical rabbinic practice on its head. Instead of sifting among 'applicants,' Jesus took the initiative to command people to follow Him. And, unlike the prophets who pointed people to God, Jesus pointed people to Himself."[53]

---

[51]Neudecker, "Master-Disciple...," 255.

[52]Andreas J. Köstenberger, "Jesus as Rabbi in the Fourth Gospel" *Bulletin for Biblical Research* 8:1 (1998): 97-128.

[53]Craig Blomberg, *Jesus and the Gospels* (Nashville, TN: Broadman & Holman, 1997), 234.

Jesus' ministry was built around His relationships with the apostles. As He explained to them,

> *"No longer do I call you servants, for the servant does not know what his master is doing; but I have called you friends, for all that I have heard from my Father I have made known to you. You did not choose me, but I chose you and appointed you that you should go and bear fruit and that your fruit should abide, so that whatever you ask the Father in my name, he may give it to you."*
> (John 15:15-16)

Their relationship was deeper than friendship, but it was at least that. The band of apostles did not function as a nomadic Bible study, wandering from location to location throughout Judea. Rather, they were invited into the life of Jesus with great intimacy. There are multiple instances where Jesus seemingly responds to them with humor or sarcasm. While Jesus taught the masses, He explained the meaning of parables only to His disciples (Matthew 13:10-17). Jesus' approach to the apostles set the stage for later patterns of relational discipleship among Christians, and it is imperative to recognize the ways it is anchored in (and different from) His contemporaries.

It is indisputable that Jesus' contemporaries saw Him as a rabbi, even while He seemed to redefine the rabbi/disciple relationship. What is less clear is precisely how much Jesus' rabbinic approach reflects the common practices of His day. Despite affirming the two primary distinctions noted above, Köstenberger explains,

> Since Judaism did not compile its traditions systematically in written form until the end of the second century AD, and since pre-AD 70 Judaism was characterized by comparatively greater variety than its later counterpart, Rabbinic Judaism (post-AD

70), it is difficult to secure reliable background information for first-century AD rabbi-disciple relations.[54]

This makes it difficult to confidently determine how much Jesus' approach to discipleship reflected or diverged from His contemporaries. The Gospels continually refer to Jesus as "Rabbi." The Gospels of Mark and John call Jesus "Rabbi" four and nine times respectively. In Mark 9:5, during the Transfiguration, Peter calls Jesus "Rabbi." Judas calls Jesus "Rabbi" in Matthew 26:25 when he betrays Jesus in the Garden of Gethsemane. Perhaps the most memorable of all the times Jesus is called "Rabbi" is John 20:16 when Mary first recognizes Jesus after He has risen from the grave and declares, "Rabboni," which is an affectionate way of saying, "My master!" It is accurate to conclude, "Jesus was, perhaps more, but certainly no less, than a rabbi."[55]

The "tradition of the elders" Jesus accuses the Pharisees of placing as more authoritative than Scripture is likely the teaching of the Mishna quoted above. Matthew 15 demonstrates that even though there is a gap between the time of Jesus and the time when the Mishna was written down, the teachings of the Mishna were certainly prevalent during Jesus' life. Jesus did not reject all the teachings of the Mishna, but He did rebuk the Pharisees for honoring their Oral Tradition above the Scriptures. It seems that Jesus gave His own interpretation of Peah 1:1 when He said,

> *"Do you think that I have come to give peace on earth? No, I tell you, but rather division. For from now on in one house there will be five divided, three against two and two against three. They will be divided, father against son and son against father, mother against*

---

[54]Köstenberger, "Jesus as Rabbi...," 101. The key difference between pre-AD 70 and post is the natural result of the Jerusalem Temple being destroyed in that year.
[55]Ibid, 99.

daughter and daughter against mother, mother-in-law against her daughter-in-law and daughter-in-law against mother-in-law."

(Luke 12:51-53)

Jesus called His disciples to follow after Him.[56] This study has demonstrated many of the similarities (personal commitment, private teaching, leaving all else to follow the master) as well as the differences (the authority of Jesus' teachings and His initiative in choosing the apostles).

How Old Were the Apostles?

Much has been written about the Apostles, yet surprisingly little attention has been given to their ages when they became Jesus' disciples. For example, A. B. Bruce's *The Training of the Twelve* and John MacArthur's *Twelve Ordinary Men* provide great insight into the lives and character of each of the Apostles, but fails to address their ages.[57] This type of oversight regarding their age is fairly common because there is not much explicit detail in Scripture that shines a clear light on this question. Instead, implicit evidence is required to discern a probable age-range.

Luke 3:23 clearly says Jesus was "about 30 years of age" when He began His public ministry. This is in line with common Rabbinic practice, which stated Rabbis may take on disciples at 30 years of age. It would be extremely unlikely for Jesus, especially as a young Rabbi, to take on disciples who are older than Himself. David Macleod writes, while also noting that Christianity has always been a movement primar-

---

[56]The twelve apostles were selected from among the larger crowd of disciples who traveled with Jesus. For the purpose of this book, the "disciples" and "apostles" will be used synonymously.

[57]Alexander Balmain Bruce, *The Training of the Twelve* (New Canaan, CT: Keats Publishing, 1979). John MacArthur, *Twelve Ordinary Men: How the Master Shaped His Disciples for Greatness, and What He Wants to Do with You* (Nashville, TN: Nelson Books, 2002).

ily driven by young people, "Most of the apostles were probably still in their twenties when they went to join Jesus."[58] He points to the Apostle's youth by highlighting such passages where Jesus refers to them as "children" (τέκνα, *tekna*), "little children" (τεκνία, *teknia*), and "my dear children" (παιδία, *paidia*).[59] It would be highly offensive to refer to one's peers or elders in this way, and this makes is nearly certain that Jesus was addressing people younger than Himself. Again, considering the teaching of *Avot 5:1* regarding the age at which young men would become disciples of a rabbi, it is most probable that the disciples were in their late-teens through early-twenties. Additionally, the behavior of the disciples (wanting Jesus to call down fire on those who reject Him, arguing about who will be the greatest in the kingdom of Heaven, and being generally dull toward the more nuanced teachings of Jesus) seems like the immaturity that would correspond with the disciples as adolescents.

Furthermore, most Evangelical scholars agree the Apostle John wrote the book of Revelation under the terrorizing reign of Emperor Domitian (Ad 95-96). This date places the writing of Revelation nearly 70 years after the death of Jesus, which took place after three years of public ministry and would require John to be 100 years old if he was thirty when he began following Jesus. A younger age for John, who is widely considered the youngest of the apostles, would place him at 15 years old when he became a disciple and at 85 years old when he wrote Revelation. Considering that John and James (who were brothers) were

---

[58]David J. Macleod, "The Year of Public Favor, Part 4: The Twelve Apostles (Matthew 10:1–4; Mark 3:13–19; Luke 6:12–16) 1." *Emmaeus Journal*, 13 (2004): 27. Macleod quotes from Stewart, *The Life and Teaching of Jesus Christ*, 55-56.

[59]Mark 10:24, John 13:33, John 21:5.

also Jesus' cousins,[60] this young age becomes increasingly credible since their mother, Salome, was entrusting young John to his responsible older cousin, Jesus.

The Apostle Peter, on the other hand, is continually the default leader of the apostles. The most natural reason for this would be if he is the oldest. The Synoptic Gospels all give account of Jesus coming to Peter's house where He heals Peter's mother-in-law of a fever.[61] Peter is the only disciple who is explicitly mentioned as being married. In Matthew 17:24-27, when Peter asks Jesus how they will pay the Temple Tax required for all Jewish men over the age of 20, Jesus miraculously provides the appropriate amount, but only for Himself and Peter. It is unwise to draw conclusions by arguments from silence (other disciples could have been married and over the age of 20 but simply were not mentioned in that account), but Peter is consistently portrayed in the Gospels as the oldest and most senior disciple.

The manner in which some other apostles were called to become disciples indicates they would be growing into adulthood. Matthew was a Tax Collector and had his own tax booth. Andrew and Simon Peter were disciples of John the Baptist before they followed Jesus. The other Simon is consistently referred to as "Simon the Zealot," which points to his involvement in a movement that sought Israel's liberation from Roman rule. Aside from the accounts of their calling to follow Jesus, we are not given much detail about their stages of life. Other apostles are simply introduced into the storyline of the Gospels with no background given. The silence regarding marital status of all the apostles

---

[60]This is a common view but not universal. Evidence is found in Matthew 27:55-56, Mark 15:40, and John 19:25. This family relationship also sheds light on the bold request made by James and John's mother (Jesus' aunt) in Matthew 20:21, that her sons (Jesus' cousins) would be given special honor when Jesus enters into His kingdom as well as Jesus' request in John 19:25-27 that John would take care of His mother, Mary.
[61]Matthew 8:14-15, Mark 1:29-31, Luke 4:38-41.

except Peter is noteworthy, since Avot 5:1 expected most Jewish men to begin pursuing marriage at eighteen years old.

Given what is known about contemporary Rabbinic practices and the above-mentioned circumstantial evidence, it seems most probable that the apostles were young adults ranging from 15 years old to late-twenties. It would be dishonest to label Jesus as "the first youth pastor," but it is undeniable that Jesus focused His ministry to the next generation and called them to leave their families in order to follow Him. In modern times, the disciples would have all been labeled "young adults," and it is important to acknowledge that even in Jesus' day, these men were still considered relatively young. The band of disciples represent Jesus' drive to build up young leaders who will carry the message of the gospel after He ascended (see John 14). Donald MacLeod observes, "God does use the young, and, in fact, many pioneer ventures and efforts that break out of established ministries and churches are spearheaded by the young. The ministry of Jesus was just such a pioneer effort."[62]

Youth Ministry Beyond the Gospels

Households in the New Testament

The New Testament occasionally references households in ways that helpfully sheds light upon the continuity regarding family discipleship in the Old Covenant and in the New. Understanding the meaning of "household" is most relevant concerning interpretations of household baptisms and spiritual leadership in the home. The Greek οἶκος (*oíkos*) is typically translated as "house" or "home" because it points to a physical building where a family lives (or the temple, which may be considered the "house of God"). But there are instances when it is used

---

[62]Macleod, "The Year of Public Favor...," 29.

symbolically of the household or family. Those latter uses are worthy of exploration in this chapter.

"Household" is a broad and symbolic translation for οἶκος in many circumstances. Paul notably writes in Ephesians 2:19, *"So then you are no longer strangers and aliens, but you are fellow citizens with the saints and members of the household of God."* In this passage, the family is used as Paul's metaphor of choice when describing Christians' new identity. However, οἶκος is not only used in reference to Christians. The Jewish people are in mind when Jesus talks about the "house of Israel" (Matthew 10:6, 15:24) and other Scriptures use οἶκος in a way that is clearly representative of a group of people (Acts 7:10; Hebrews 3:6). The symbolic, corporate identity in mind in passages where οἶκος is used in the singular form (Matthew 10:6, 15:24; Acts 7:10; Ephesians 2:19) and in plural (1 Timothy 3:15; 1 Peter 4:17), thus translation and interpretation remains somewhat vague and depends primarily on exegetical context rather than lexical form. The grammatical form οἰκία generally points to a more literal family.[63] With this broader understanding of οἶκος in the New Testament, it is worth remembering that the biblical view of family and household was much broader than the modern conception of the nuclear family. Instead, there is an emphasis on corporate identity rather than individual identity.

Household baptisms (Acts 16:31, 18:8; 1 Corinthians 1:16) are important to consider. However, because of the emphasis of this book, the emphasis remains on implications regarding ministry to the next generation rather than any attempt to settle the baptism debate. Regardless of one's view on infant baptism or believer's baptism, it is the ordinance or sacrament to mark entrance into the Church. Those who hold to believer's baptism view it as a public declaration of one's conversion and rebirth as a child of God: an outward demonstration of

---

[63] O. Michel "οἶκος οἰκία," *Theological Dictionary of the New Testament*, vol. 5 (Grand Rapids, MI: Eerdmans, 1967), 129-34.

what has happened spiritually. Paedobaptists believe circumcision has been replaced by baptism as the sign of the covenant and therefore infants receive the mark of baptism as an expression of their identity as a child of the covenant. In both views, baptism is symbolic of one's identity as a child of God. The reason this is relevant is because whether or not these households were a biological family (children included) or a broader representation of one's clan, these references highlight the ongoing call to family discipleship in the new covenant. When the head of the household was converted it marked a change for the entire household because he understood his spiritual responsibility for those under his authority.

Ephesians 2:19 and similar passages make it clear that Christians belong to a new household of faith. As members of the family of God, there is a biblical mandate for spiritual parents to disciple the next generation. The New Testament references to οἶκος emphasizes that Christians are members of the household of God, not only to their biological family. The spiritually mature become a kind of "faith parent" to those who are younger. More will be said about this in later chapters, but an exegetical word-study on οἶκος contributes to the discussion surrounding intergenerational discipleship in the church and in the home.

Titus 2:1-7

Titus 2 presents one of the only direct and explicit commands, in the New Testament, for the older generations to disciple the younger generation. It is important to recognize the biblical context for this call to intergenerational discipleship. Paul begins this exhortation with a general call to teach sound doctrine, as opposed to those who teach false doctrine, and then tells older men and older women that he expects them to set an example of godliness. The calling to disciple and mentor those who are younger goes hand in hand with the church's commitment to doctrinal purity. After all, if teachers in the church are living faithless or hypocritical lives it is a great scar on the content of their teaching.

It is unfortunate how many pastors today give themselves to careful preaching of the Word but delegate discipleship of the next generation to volunteers or younger pastors entirely. Titus 2:1-7 makes it clear that intergenerational discipleship must be a priority among mature Christians. When younger Christians are not discipled and are overlooked by the mature believers, there should be no surprise when the church's reputation suffers among nonbelievers. Pastors have many responsibilities, and it seems like every pastoral leadership book wants to add one more onto their plate, but it is surely unbiblical and foolish to overlook this important task. Even where a church has a staff of full-time youth ministers, the church's pastors and elders are the spiritual leaders of the church, including the young. Even though leadership of the younger generations may be delegated and entrusted to someone else, the pastor must not be absent and disconnected from the children and youth in the church.

It is somewhat disappointing that many seem to only focus on Paul's exhortations to older women, while overlooking verse 6, *"Likewise, urge the younger men to be self-controlled."* Interestingly, ὡσαύτως *(hōsaútōs,* typically translated as "likewise" or "in the same way") is not the first word in the Greek text of verse 6. Instead, "the younger men"[64] begins the verse, preceding ὡσαύτως for the sake of emphasis. This highlights that the same commands that applied to older women's responsibilities with younger women also applies to the younger men. Women are not the only ones who are called to disciple those who are younger. Paul's instructions to Titus are clear: the older and more mature need to take initiative in training the younger and less mature so the Church would

---

64Τοὺς νεωτέρους (*Tous neōterous*)

be built up, Christ would be exalted, and the next generation would grow into Christian maturity.

The Apostle Paul as Mentor

The Apostle Paul was a man with a marked past. This is something today's Christians hear on occasion, but easily gloss over. Paul, then called Saul, directly oversaw the death of Stephen, the first Christian martyr. Paul's own conversion took place while he was actively seeking the imprisonment and death of Christians. He was the primary opponent of the gospel for the earliest Christians. Even with such untrustworthy a resume, Barnabas served as Paul's mentor and vouched for his genuine conversion when others were skeptical (Acts 9:27). Paul stands as the most prominent early Christian missionary, and while that is true, it is essential to recognize that Paul was initially sent out as Barnabas' assistant. In many ways, he was mentored and discipled by Barnabas before their contentious split in Acts 15:39. Even though nothing is known of Barnabas' age, his influence as a mentor to Paul should not be overlooked in how it shaped Paul's commitment to passing the faith from generation to generation.

When considering the men whom the Apostle Paul discipled and mobilized for ministry it is helpful to remember that he was trained in the same Rabbinic tradition that was outlined earlier in this chapter. It is not difficult to imagine that Paul would select disciples who would be labeled as "youth" or "young adults" today in order that his mission to the Gentiles would continue long after his own death (and it did!).

When Barnabas and Paul were sent out from Antioch for their first missionary journey they were assisted by the young John Mark (Acts 12:25, 13:5), who eventually became a wedge between them. It is not clear how young John Mark was, but it seems obvious he was still a younger man and was presumably invited because he was Barnabas' cousin (Colossians 4:10). Regarding John Mark's contentious departure in Acts 13:13, I. Howard Marshall observes, "We simply are not told [why he returned to Jerusalem], but it is clear from 15:38 that Paul regarded his defection as a serious matter, while Barnabas was prepared to make allowances for him."[65] This seems like a situation most youth pastors have encountered: a young Christian who may not have been ready for the challenge is struggling, while older and more mature Christians disagree about how to best lead the younger believer. Barnabas departed to minister in his homeland of Cyprus with John Mark while Paul returned to Syria and Cilicia with Silas. In the end, this is the same John Mark who authored the Gospel of Mark, widely considered the earliest canonical gospel, and whom Paul wants by his side as he nears his own death (2 Timothy 4:11).

Silas was one of the "leading men among the brothers" in the Jerusalem Church (15:22). It is not entire clear if he was a Gentile or a Hellenistic Jew, but he is referred to as Silas (Greek) or Silvanus[66] (Latin) but never a Hebrew name. While it is possible he was a Gentile Christian from Jerusalem, it is far more likely he was a Hellenized Jew who was a Roman citizen.[67] This positions him as a wise advocate between the Jewish believers and the Gentile Christians, which also helps explain why he was listed as one of the official representatives who would bring the report from the Council of Jerusalem to the church in Antioch, Syria, and Cilicia (Acts 15:22-23). Silas joins Paul and Barnabas on their missionary journey when he made such a strong impression on Paul that he was chosen to remain with Paul while Barnabas and John Mark went their own way (Acts 15:40). Indeed, Acts 15:32 indicates that Silas and Judas (who was also appointed by the church in Jerusalem along with Silas) were prophets who were gifted preachers. Paul

---

[65]I. Howard Marshall, *Acts: An Introduction and Commentary*, Tyndale New Testament Commentaries, vol. 5 (Downers Grove, IL: InterVarsity Press, 1980), 222.

[66]See 2 Cor. 1:19; 1 Thess. 1:1; 2 Thess. 1:1; 1 Pet. 5:12.

[67]R. C. Campbell, "Silas" *The International Standard Bible Encyclopedia*, vol. 4 (Grand Rapids, MI: Eerdmans, 1979), 509.

and Silas were ministry partners, and although age is never specified their collaboration shows Paul's commitment to continue in others what Barnabas had done for him. Similarly with Titus and Timothy, no spouse or family is mentioned, which would have been the expected course for a mature adult. These men's status as unmarried does seem to indicate they were young men who were taken under Paul's tutelage as young ministers-in-training.

Paul demonstrated a similar relationship with Titus as he did with Silas. Galatians 2:1 introduces Titus as a Gentile convert who became a mature Christian under Paul and Barnabas' ministry. Titus is explicitly said to have been an uncircumcised Gentile (Galatians 2:3), and yet he played a vital role in the early church, especially in Crete, where he was designated as the leading pastor (Titus 1:5). Galatians 2:1-3 gives the indication that he was a young man who was converted from Paul and Barnabas' ministry and was identified as someone who would be useful in their ongoing ministry. They also selected him to be introduced to the Christians in Jerusalem as an example of God's work among the Gentiles. Throughout Paul's letters, Titus appears as a reliable companion and trustworthy partner in ministry. Titus was certainly not raised in a Christian household, thus Paul and Barnabas' ministry efforts to him mirror the evangelism and discipleship many youth pastors exhibit toward non-Christian teenagers who are receptive to the gospel.

Similarly, Timothy is portrayed as a young man who has been discipled by Paul and entrusted with significant ministry responsibilities. Paul famously refers to Timothy as "my true child in the faith" (1 Timothy 1:2) and encourages him, "let no one despise you for your youth" (1 Timothy 4:12). He is introduced in Acts 16:1-5 as "the son of a Jewish woman who was a believer, but his father was a Greek." His mother and grandmother were likely converted when Paul's first missionary journey brought him through Lystra, where he healed a crippled man and Paul and Barnabas were nicknamed Zeus and Hermes only to have an angry mob turn the crowd against them (Acts 14:8-20). By the time Paul returned to Lystra in the second missionary journey, Timothy was most likely a teenager or in his early twenties and was well-respected for his faith. It seems reliable to discern he was not a child, since he was *"well spoken of by the brothers at Lystra and Iconium"* (Acts 16:2), but neither is he presented as a mature man since it would be unusual to introduce a grown man by first mentioning his parents. When it was time for Paul and Barnabas to depart, Timothy was circumcised and brought with them as a new member of their ministry team. Timothy's father was likely deceased by this point in his life,[68] presumably with Paul filling a surrogate-father type of role that is common among youth workers in today's church.

Paul's Instructions to Children in Ephesians 6:1 & Colossians 3:20

What is notable about these sections for this book is that they were included in Paul's letters at all. It is important to remember the epistles were not written to be read silently in the privacy of each person's home, but to be read aloud when the faithful met together for worship. These portions of Paul's letters demonstrate that children were present in the fellowship of believers. The Greek construction Τὰ τέκνα (*Ta tekna*) is rendered "Children," in most English translations. This was a clear subject heading meant to address a particular group of people who were present in the assembly. If this was intended as mere instruction, Paul would have likely written, "Children should obey..." – without the definite article (Τὰ), and the verb "obey," ὑπακούετε (*hypakouete*),

---

[68]Although Timothy's mother was Jewish, he had not been circumcised according to Jewish custom. This would indicate that his Gentile father was opposed to the practice, and yet the text is silent regarding his father's opinion about Timothy's circumcision in verse 3. His father is never mentioned anywhere else in Scripture, although his mother and grandmother are referred to in 2 Timothy 1:5, which indicates that Paul never met Timothy's father. Elsewhere, Paul encourages Christian wives to submit to their non-Christian husbands, so it would be out of character for Paul to urge Timothy to completely overlook his father's will if he was alive.

would have been in the Subjunctive case rather than the Imperative. Ephesians 6:1 and Colossians 3:20 make two things clear regarding children in the life of the church: first, the children are present among the faithful in worship, and second, Paul wrote his letters with the next generation in mind. In these ways, Paul continues the Old Testament emphasis on training the next generation in the fear of the Lord.

Conclusion: Youth Ministry in the New Testament

The above survey has presented an overwhelming case for the value of ministry to the next generation. It is notable that, to a significant degree, Christianity was established by unmarried men who began their ministries at a younger age than most modern-day churches would want for a senior pastor: Jesus, the Apostles, Paul, Timothy, Silas, and others. As God in flesh, Jesus could have selected any group of people to become His disciples but He chose a group of teenagers and young adults who were overwhelmingly ordinary. Jesus spent time with His young apostles and empowered them for significant ministry, entrusting them with the mission of the Church. In a similar way that Jesus called and trained disciples, the Apostle Paul intentionally trained Silas, Timothy, and Titus as evangelists and church planters.

Many books on family ministry seem to overlook the New Testament frameworks for family discipleship and intergenerational ministry in the Church, which runs deeper than Jesus permitting the little children to come to Him (Matthew 19:14) and for older women to train the younger women to become godly wives (Titus 2:3-4). As will be seen in chapter 4, Church History reflects the New Testament's teaching on establishing faithful elders who will teach and disciple not only the adults, but also the children. Whether one looks to Jesus' rabbinic ministry with the disciples or at other examples throughout the

New Testament, there is a consistent legacy of godly adults ministering to the young and raising them up to be leaders in the church.

Where family discipleship is commanded in the Old Testament, it is displayed in the New Testament through the context of the Church as the family of God. This theme will be further elaborated in Chapter 5, but it is important to see a consistent pattern throughout Scripture. Christians must be people who read the whole Bible through a lens of gospel-centered biblical theology. Jesus' own ministry is a picture of intergenerational ministry, as is Paul's. Meanwhile the brief glimpses of households confessing faith in Jesus in Acts also reflects the family's ongoing calling to family discipleship. One of the key emphases that modern youth ministry and church leaders should take from the New Testament is the priority given to passing the faith to the next generation and then raising them into leadership in the church. Too many teenagers are given the impression that serving in the church means serving in the youth or children's ministries. Rather than viewing children and youth as "members in waiting," the biblical witness consistently affirms their value and reflects a shared commitment by the community of faith toward the next generation. Pastors and Christian leaders today who overlook the young are in blatant disregard of the biblical pattern of ministry.

Chapter 4

Church History and Youth Ministry

The church has always had church kids. Who has ministered to them throughout history? Adolescence has changed, but there has always been the need for parents and leaders in the church to evangelize and disciple the next generation. Every culture is different and the centuries have brought about remarkable changes even within those cultures, so it should be obvious that ministry to teenagers would look different than it does today. And yet there is a central thread that runs throughout the Church's ministry to those who are growing from childhood into adulthood. Today's youth workers are not the first generation to consider how to minister to teenagers.

The method employed throughout most of church history until modern times is called catechesis. A basic survey of church history will show that the Church has often faced the challenge of discipling new Christians in a culture that was opposed to the Christian faith. This is not a uniquely modern challenge the Church faces, and wisdom would lead church leaders to consider how this challenge has been addressed in the past. Gary Parrett and Steve Kang reflect on the Church's legacy being preserved by catechesis when they write, "The ministry of catechesis was the cornerstone of educational practices in the church during the first several centuries following the New Testament era and again from the Reformation period and on through the times of the Puritans both in England and in America."[69]

In *Grounded in the Gospel*, J. I. Packer and Gary Parrett present a compelling argument for catechesis in the church's history and how catechesis can serve as a faithful guide to building believers today.[70] Throughout church history, catechesis has continually emphasized instruction on the Ten Commandments, the Apostle's Creed, the Lord's Prayer, and the sacraments/ordinances of the Church.[71] The three major periods throughout church history in which catechesis was particularly emphasized were in the second through fifth century of the Early Church, during the Reformation in the sixteenth century, and then again among the English Puritans of the seventeenth century. These three periods will be briefly explored prior to setting a historical context for the development of modern youth ministry.

Catechesis in the Early Church

The first generation of Christians were considered a sect of Judaism by Roman authorities. It is reasonable, then, to conclude they followed a similar pattern of education for their children as described in the Mishna. As new believers sought participation and membership in the Early Church, there were important questions pastors and church leaders needed to ask. Their challenge was to retain evangelistic zeal while practicing discernment regarding those who sought to persecute them by gaining access to insider information about church members. Membership in the church frequently involved a long process because wisdom and caution needed to be practiced. The following table presents

---

[69]Gary A. Parrett and S. Steve Kang, *Teaching the Faith, Forming the Faithful: A Biblical Vision for Education in the Church* (Downers Grove, IL: IVP Academic, 2009), 89.

[70]J. I. Packer and Gary A. Parrett, *Grounded in the Gospel: Building Believers the Old-Fashioned Way* (Grand Rapids, MI: Baker Books, 2010).

[71]Ibid, 85-88.

both the structure and content of catechesis as it came to maturity under the ministry of Augustine, whose catechetical method may be considered the most developed and influential within the Early Church.[72]

Table 1: Phases of a Catechetical Journey Under the Ministry of Augustine

	Phases of a Catechetical Journey Under the Ministry of Augustine	Content Emphasis
Inquirers	Those expressing interest in the Faith.	The *narratio* (the great redemptive Story) told in compelling fashion.
Catechumens	Those newly submitted to instruction in the Faith.	A long, sustained exposure, mostly in the setting of congregational worship, to biblical instruction that was both moral and doctrinal.
Competentes	Those enrolled as candidates for baptism.	An intense time of preparation that included prayers, fasting, moral admonition, and instruction in the Creed and the Lord's Prayer.
Neophytes	Those who have just been baptized.	A first experience of the Eucharist, with instruction about the meaning and mystery of the sacraments.
The faithful	Those who have been baptized believers for some time.	Regular retelling of the redemptive Story, ongoing instruction in the Scriptures, primarily in the context of assembled worship.

Inquirers were people who desired to be taught about the Christian faith, but they needed a Sponsor who would vouch for the person's

---

[72]Ibid, 142-3. This pattern is further described in 154-7.

integrity.[73] At this point, the emphasis was beyond simply getting the inquirer to want to become a Christian (what is typically thought of as evangelism today). Instead, it was viewed as a time-consuming and important component of discipleship where a Christian worldview was taught.[74] This led to converts entering into the faith with a robust understanding of Scripture and what it meant to be a Christian. When the Inquirer had been taught the basic truths of the biblical narrative, if the catechist approved, the Inquirer would then become a *Catechumen*. Catechumens would continue to be formally trained in Christian doctrine while beginning to share in the church's worship but not yet in the Lord's Supper; they would, in fact, be dismissed from gathered worship before the Lord's Supper was celebrated.[75] After Catechumens had grown in both knowledge of doctrine and in godliness, they would become candidates for baptism, formally called *Competentes*. This stage of catechesis typically occurred during the season of Lent and entailed more formal discipleship by the pastor or bishop, daily prayers, ascetic practices, and even prayers of exorcism.[76] Most importantly, it was during this stage that Competentes would learn the Creed orally and would be required to memorize it line by line and repeat it back to his or her instructor.[77] After baptism, the catechetical process typically drew to a close as the new Neophyte would receive further instructions regarding explanations about baptism's symbolism or any other doctrinal matters that were kept hidden until the candidate had been baptized.[78]

From this outline above, it is clear that the Early Church took a proactive role in both evangelism and in the discipleship of new believers.

---

[73]Ibid, 54.
[74]See Parrett and Kang, *Teaching the Faith, Forming the Faithful*, 132-135.
[75]Packer and Parrett, *Grounded in the Gospel*, 54.
[76]Ibid, 55.
[77]Ibid, 55.
[78]Ibid, 57.

The road to baptism sometimes took years, depending upon the individual's progress, but it is evident that there were structures and processes in place throughout the Church, though it varied slightly from church to church. It must be noted the catechetical journey was a highly-relational process where the catechist and the one being catechized would develop a deep bond of trust and faith as they discussed both Christian doctrine and the Christian life. The notion that catechesis was impersonal because of the high level of structure is completely inaccurate and must be dismissed.

One outstanding question that remains to be thoroughly researched is this: who catechized the church kids? The catechetical process was largely evangelistic and involved the spiritual development of converts. What remains unclear is the process of church membership and baptism for children of Christians in the Early Church. The Didache makes it clear that the earliest form of baptism more closely resembled believer's baptism rather than infant baptism.[79] When unbaptized children grew up and wanted to pursue baptism, who walked them through the catechetical process? This is a largely unaddressed question, both in primary resources and in church history books. After consulting with numerous scholars, it is most likely that while parents were charged with catechesis at home, a catechist from the church (not their father) would have led in discipleship as the adolescent prepared for baptism. It is likely the Early Church trained catechists to serve as youth workers who would come alongside parents in ministry to their children as they transitioned into adulthood (symbolized by baptism). This is a topic that requires significant research.

---

[79]Everett Ferguson, *Baptism in the Early Church: History, Theology, and Liturgy in the First Five Centuries* (Grand Rapids, MI: William B. Eerdmans Pub. Co., 2009).

Catechesis in the Reformation

The Reformation was a time of great biblical and doctrinal renewal, not only in the church but also in the home. Parents were affirmed as the chief catechists in the home, and the reformers held negligent parents to account for their failure to intentionally teach their children "by explicit and systematic examination and exposition."[80] Correcting this absence of family discipleship was the primary reason the reformers placed such heavy emphasis on developing new catechisms. Catechesis experienced such a great revival that Packer and Parrett have exclaimed, "it could well be argued that the Reformation itself was a response to centuries of catechetical decline."[81]

While most people had not been clearly and practically instructed in the gospel and sound doctrine, and whereas the Bible itself had been inaccessible to the overwhelming majority of people, the Reformation ushered in a new season when catechesis would return in force. Luther availed himself of the opportunities for broad distribution through the printing press in order to publish both his small and large catechisms in 1529. Luther clarified his motivations in printing the catechisms by writing, "The common people, especially those who live in the country, have no knowledge whatever of Christian teaching, and unfortunately many pastors are quite incompetent and unfitted for teaching."[82] These written catechisms provided both parents and pastors with a doctrinally rich resource that was simple to use with children. Since the parents were now instructed to take up the task themselves, Luther provided a resource whereby the parents received doctrinal instruction even as they taught their children.

---

[80]William Haugaard, "The Continental Reformation of the Sixteenth Century," ed. O. C. Edwards Jr & John H. Westerhoff III, *A Faithful Church: Issues in the History of Catechesis*, (Eugene, OR: Wipf and Stock, 2003), 135.
[81]Packer & Parrett, *Grounded in the Gospel*, 59.
[82]As quoted Ibid, 61.

Previous generations of catechists depended upon verbal teaching and repetition. Luther is responsible for the question-and-answer format that has become practically synonymous with catechesis.[83] He chose the question-and-answer structure for its clarity and ease of use for parents. Luther's catechisms contained the traditional content in expositing the Ten Commandments, the Apostle's Creed, the Lord's Prayer, and an interpretation of the sacraments of the Church; most subsequent catechisms have also shared these emphases, though the order may vary.[84]

In the midst of such a clear and powerful call for parents to lead in catechizing their children, Luther remained committed to seeing the local church as the primary spiritual influence, while the family's discipleship is also reinforced through public education. Parents were the primary disciplers of their children, but the church leaders were the primary spiritual leaders of the family. He repeatedly argued for the necessity of public education for children and believed that should also include spiritual matters.[85] Regarding those who disciple other people's children, Luther writes, "It surely has to be one of the supreme virtues on earth faithfully to train other people's children: for there are very few people, in fact, almost none, who will do this for their own."[86] The reformers did not eschew educational models of their day. Instead, they built upon them for the sake of educating the next generation of faithful Christians even while affirming the primary role of parents.

John Calvin shared this commitment to catechesis at home while setting up an even more structured educational system in Geneva than Luther promoted in Germany. Calvin's commitment to schooling did not mean he was shifting spiritual responsibility from parents onto the

---

[83] Ibid, 191.
[84] Ibid, 62.
[85] Haugaard, 136-8.
[86] As quoted in, Haugaard, 138.

educational institution, but it is clear he believed the parent's calling to disciple children would be reinforced, instead of usurped, by partnership with other adults in their children's education and formation.[87]

Given the great amount of doctrinal writings that were published, it should be no surprise that one of the Reformation's greatest contributions to catechesis has been a prolific amount of written catechisms. The Reformers consistently urged parents to be catechizing their children while affirming the Church's calling to lead in the gospel. Parents were encouraged to pursue both discipleship at home and to avail themselves of opportunities for their children to be shaped through other educational resources.

Catechesis Among the Puritans

The Puritans, who emerged during the English Reformation, are best known for their firm commitment to doctrine, but it must be remembered they were also greatly committed to godliness. This dual commitment is seen clearly through their teachings on parents' responsibility to their children. Matthew Henry strongly urged both parents and ministers to be actively committed to the catechizing of children.[88] J. C. Ryle's *Thoughts for Young Men* is still widely read and circulated, and was written to give practical counsel for youth.[89] Jonathan Edwards' ministry to the youth in Northampton has been referred to as the spark that set flame to the Great Awakening.[90] This is all to highlight that the Puritan ministers were committed to raising up the next generation in the love and fear of the LORD. Richard Baxter is most commonly associated with the Puritans' practice of catechesis and often serves as

---

[87]Ibid, 141-2.
[88]Matthew Henry, *Family Religion: Principles for Raising a Godly Family* (Fearn, Ross-shire, Scotland: Christian Heritage, 2008), 92-94.
[89]J. C. Ryle, *Thoughts for Young Men* (United States: Renaissance Classics, 2012).
[90]George Marsden, *Jonathan Edwards: A Life* (New Haven, CT: Yale, 2003), 150-1.

their exemplar; thus his ministry is highlighted as the most prominent example.

Baxter felt so strongly about the necessity of family ministry that he very pointedly wrote, "Good laws will not reform us, if reformation begin not at home.... I beseech you, therefore, if you desire the reformation and welfare of your people, do all you can to promote family religion."[91] Prior to his ministry in the city of Kidderminster, the people had a terrible reputation and the Church of England received so many complaints about their minister that he was replaced by Baxter, then only twenty-five years old. He preached twice each week and set aside two entire days to visit families so he could test them on the sermon's content and on their understanding of the catechism. According to Baxter himself,

> "On the Lord's days there was no disorder to be seen in the streets, but you might hear a hundred families singing psalms and repeating sermons as you passed through the streets. In a word, when I came thither first, there was about one family in a street that worshipped God and called on his name. When I came away there were some streets where there was not more than one family in the side of a street that did not so."[92]

He labored for the gospel in Kidderminster for fifteen years with such fruitfulness that eighty-three years after his tenure George Whitefield remarked, "I was greatly refreshed to find what a sweet savour of good Mr. Baxter's doctrine, works and discipline remain to this day."[93]

---

[91] Richard Baxter, *The Saints' Everlasting Rest*, Select Works of Richard Baxter. Accordance electronic ed. (Altamonte Springs, FL: OakTree Software, 2006), n.p.

[92] As quoted in Maurice Roberts, "Richard Baxter and His Gospel" *Banner of Truth Magazine*, 339, December 1991, accessed July 21, 2013, http://www.puritansermons.com/baxter/baxter19.htm."

[93] Ibid.

Baxter's vision for family religion was the heart that drove his practice of catechesis. In his conversations with families, he also tested and taught the children during these home visits. Had he relied solely on his sermons or on various church-based programs to catechize the families, then it is doubtful Whitefield's comment about Kidderminster would ever have been made. The families of Kidderminster were not particularly "ripe" for the task of discipleship, but through diligence and perseverance Baxter literally found doors slowly opening to him as he preached and catechized. Kidderminster was transformed for generations because of Baxter's faithfulness to the gospel and his commitment to seeing it take root in parents and their children.

It is notable that upon taking up the mantle as pastor in Kidderminster, Baxter gave himself to the preaching of Scripture and to family discipleship. Baxter trained other ministers and elders to share in this responsibility, but not as a means for him to delegate the task to others so he could tend to more important matters. He stands above other Puritans in his practice of door-to-door catechesis with families, but this emphasis is present throughout many of the Puritans.

The Development of Modern Youth Ministry

There has always been a season of transition from childhood into adulthood. Whether this season should be called "adolescence" throughout history or not is up for debate,[94] but a transition into adulthood is not a newly formed social construct. What is new is its indeterminate length of adolescence and the youth culture that has arisen to support and prolong it. Crystal Kirgiss makes the argument in her book, *In Search of Adolescence*, "For most of history, with some variations here and there as societies went through significant changes or upheav-

---

[94]David F. White, "The Social Construction of Adolescence," in Brian J. Mahan, Michael Warren, David F. White, *Awakening Youth Discipleship: Christian Resistance in a Consumer Culture* (Eugene, OR: Wipf and Stock, 2008), 3-19

al, there was a very clear understanding of a stage of life that followed childhood and preceded adulthood."[95] While adolescence is not entirely new, it would be foolish and irresponsible to equate the adolescent's experience in history with today's counterpart. Among the most objective measurements of adolescence throughout history is the age when girls begin menstruation, known as menarche. Walt Mueller observes, "The average age for when a girl first menstruates is twelve years and nine months. One hundred years ago, this usually happened two and a half years later—when a girl was 15."[96] Despite the differences, this history shows the reality that the church has always needed to work with parents to guide "church kids" from childhood into adulthood, and that process did not happen overnight.

Whether the generation following World War II marked the beginning of adolescence itself or simply a new kind of adolescence, it is indisputable that this season marked the advent of "youth culture." The creation of a sub-culture for those who are no longer children but not yet adults provided the social context for adolescence to expand both earlier and later in life. This new era in child development created seismic ripples throughout culture. Delayed adulthood shifted the age of marriage from the mid-teens to the late-teens and finally to late-twenties today. Whereas children were previously guided through adolescence as quickly and clearly as possible by their parents, this new season of adolescence meant teenagers were given freedom to embrace the transitional season of life while continuing as dependents. Teenagers now had their own peer groups at school, their own music, movies, and television shows. Once advertisers realized teenagers also had access to disposable money, the marketing and products created specifically

---

[95]Crystal Kirgiss, *In Search of Adolescence: A New Look at an Old Idea* (San Diego, CA: The Youth Cartel, 2015), 35.
[96]Walt Mueller, *The Space Between: a Parent's Guide to Teenage Development* (Grand Rapid, MI.: Zondervan, 2009), 38.

for adolescents exponentially multiplied. In recent years, the internet and ease of access to handheld technology has only compounded the increasing separation of youth culture from the broader culture.

Modern youth ministry came of age in this post World War II culture. As these teenagers experienced unprecedented freedom without the previous generations' responsibilities, churches struggled to know how to respond. Parents seemed to be taking an increasingly passive role in their teenagers' lives. A highly private generation of parents also meant that children rarely heard from their parents about spiritual matters. As youth culture became more widely accepted, the church struggled to discern how to respond. Elvis, the Beatles, and the "British Invasion" seemed like dangerous influences for teenagers, but the church was ill-equipped to respond with anything other than judgment and condemnation.

Mark Senter III, the author of *When God Shows Up: A History of Protestant Youth Ministry in America*, argues for four major cycles in the development of modern youth ministry.[97] The first cycle (1824-75) brought about the formation of youth ministry agencies, such as the Sunday School societies, YMCA, and temperance societies. These agencies eventually lost an emphasis on spiritual development and began to primarily emphasize right behavior. As a correction to this, the second cycle (1881-1925) sought Christian faithfulness through education as displayed through ministries like the Young People's Society of Christian Endeavor. Parachurch agencies like Youth for Christ and Young Life embody the third cycle (1933-89) with a highly relational approach to ministry, especially toward youth who did not already attend church. Finally, Senter argues that a fourth cycle began in the 1990s, though its emphases remain unclear and are still being defined.

---

[97]Mark Senter, *When God Shows Up: a History of Protestant Youth Ministry in America*, Youth, Family, and Culture Series (Grand Rapids, MI: Baker Academic, 2010), xii-xiii.

This outline of the history of youth ministry is helpful, and yet it seems strange to include a fourth stage that is nearly thirty years old but still undefined and presented without a representative ministry agency. Senter's approach to the cycles seems built around the objectives of the ministries: education, right behavior, and evangelism. Instead of approaching the eras of youth ministry by objectives, this book proposed the eras should be marked according to the methods employed. Naturally, there will be significant overlap, but this seems a more natural way to think about the structural development of modern youth ministry.

The first era of modern youth ministry began in England with the first known Sunday School class that was held in 1769 by Hannah Ball, a disciple of John Wesley. This was an era marked by newfound questioning of authority. Just over a decade later, in 1780, Robert Raikes began his own Sunday School movement and provided the leadership necessary, which led to Sunday Schools becoming a common fixture in the local church. While Sunday School is now an unquestioned cornerstone of many churches that is focused on teaching the Bible and core doctrinal truths to children, it began as a widely-criticized ministry that received many condemnations from ministers throughout England. Undeterred, Raikes continued to minister to boys, describing his ministry thus, "The children were to come after ten in the morning, and stay till twelve; they were then to go home and return at one; and after reading a lesson, they were to be conducted to church. After church, they were to be employed in repeating the catechism till after five, and then dismissed, with an injunction to go home without making a noise."[98] The incredible influence of Sunday School on children and youth was unparalleled for over a century until it has waned in popularity and favor in recent years.

---

[98]Montrose J. Moses, *Children's Books and Reading* (New York, NY: Mitchell Kennerley, 1907), 103.

The growing acceptance of Sunday Schools set the stage for the formation of the Young People's Society of Christian Endeavor in 1881. Rev. Francis Edward Clark, the founder and first president of Christian Endeavor, published books and manuals specifically written for youth, urging them to grow in zeal for evangelism and serving the Lord. Suddenly, there were a growing number of efforts specifically commissioned to minister to children and youth. As Christian Endeavor and similar ministries began to grow more accepted, youth culture continued to grow deeper roots not only in the broader culture, but also in the church.

Frank Otis Erb wrote this in 1917 about the last half of the 18th Century,

> In addition to this political aspect, the democratic spirit led a revolt against absolutism everywhere, religion and intellect not excluded. The final and authoritative doctrines of the church were fiercely assailed by Voltaire and his friends, not least because they were final and authoritative, and those who held them were denounced as ignorant, superstitious, or hypocritical. Freedom of thought was not only demanded but asserted.[99]

This radical shift set the stage for future generations to question the religious beliefs of previous generations and the church needed to respond. By the time Erb was writing, this newfound philosophical freedom led to the popularity of Unitarianism while children were expected to work long hours in factories and were often illiterate. Ministries like Sunday Schools, Christian Endeavor, and the YMCA provided examples of a response whereby children were taught the Scriptures. In many ways, the development of modern youth ministry can be linked

---

[99]Frank Otis Erb, *The Development of the Young People's Movement* (Chicago, IL: University of Chicago Press, 1917), 1.

with the evolution of secularism, and this remains true in the first era of modern youth ministry.

The second era of modern youth ministry began in 1941 with the formation of Young Life by Jim Rayburn. Mark Senter makes the accurate observation that "cycles of youth ministry have usually been initiated by an event outside youth ministry that is pivotal in shaping the world of the adolescent."[100] Whereas the first era was marked by the formation of child labor laws, the second grew roots in the fertile soil of newly formed youth culture after World War II. This was a time when adolescence was expanding and teenagers were given newfound freedom to "discover themselves" as more than children but without adult responsibilities, and the Church floundered in its response. While churches discussed and debated how to respond to youth culture, parachurch organizations like Young Life, Youth For Christ (1944), and Fellowship of Christian Athletes (1954) were formed to engage students with the gospel.

Countless teenagers who would have never broached the doors of a church heard and believed in the gospel through Jim Rayburn's Young Life clubs. Non-Christian teenagers who refused to come onto church property were suddenly being introduced to Christian community and the gospel. In many ways, Young Life represents what most people think of when they hear "Youth Ministry": a program where adult leaders seek to build relationships where the gospel is proclaimed to teens through a combination of games, food, biblical teaching, and entering the teenager's turf. Instead of relying on methods employed by radio preachers and revivalism strategies, Rayburn's strategy is still the leading approach in modern youth ministry where youth workers

---

[100]Mark Senter, "A Historical Framework for Doing Youth Ministry," edited by Richard R. Dunn and Mark Senter, *Reaching a Generation for Christ: a Comprehensive Guide to Youth Ministry* (Chicago, IL: Moody Press, 1997), 107.

are viewed as missionaries to unchurched teenagers who use a conversational approach to win a hearing for the gospel.[101]

Where Young Life provided the blueprint for what many church-based youth groups would become, Youth For Christ laid the groundwork for Christian camping and retreats. Youth for Christ began their most effective evangelistic crusades in the late 1940s, launching the ministry of Billy Graham and continuing in America's Revivalist tradition of Charles Finney and Billy Sunday. Evangelistic preaching of the gospel and the use of altar calls and worship music were heavily employed as the ministry approach to invite those in attendance, who tended to be among the younger generations, to confess faith in Jesus Christ. This emphasis on large-scale rallies for students spread but have since fizzled as students grew disenchanted and began to prefer more personal settings where relationships were fostered. The legacy of these rallies, however, may be seen in the Christian camps that remain committed to providing an experience for teenagers to retreat from their day-to-day lives in order to grow in Christ.

This era is marked by newer ministry philosophies espoused by parachurch ministries that provided a template for church-based ministries to follow. As churches began to follow the models set by these parachurch ministries, youth workers were largely resourced by Youth Specialties (1969). Mike Yaconelli and Wayne Rice began producing resources to equip churches and youth workers through the ministry of Youth Specialties in the early 1970s. Although Youth Specialties formally incorporated in the late 60s, they have hosted an annual National Youth Workers Convention since 1970 and published hundreds of books, curriculum, and other resources. It is no exaggeration to say that, over the last five decades, no one has influenced youth ministry more than Youth Specialties.

---

[101]Senter, *When God Shows Up,* 263.

Throughout this second era, the various forms of youth ministry taught Scripture and focused on bringing the gospel to unchurched teenagers while emphasizing relationships over programs and conversation over teaching. They focused their attention on teenagers rather than the church, and occasionally fell into the trap of presenting itself as a cooler alternative to church. As this era progressed, many of the practices of parachurch organizations were adopted by local churches in an attempt to evangelize and disciple teenagers in their community. Integrating students into the life of the church was rarely an option for youth workers, many of whom were viewed with suspicion by church leaders, while parents were increasingly happy to delegate their spiritual authority to a new class of professional youth workers.

A third era of youth ministry has emerged over the last decade as youth workers are increasingly alarmed by the student dropout rate. Many are reconsidering whether or not modern youth ministry is a failed experiment. Wayne Rice, a co-founder of Youth Specialties, somberly reflects,

> "I have all the respect in the world for youth workers in the church, but I've become more and more convinced over the years that God never gave to youth workers the responsibility for making disciples of other people's kids.... What we have today is not really a youth ministry problem. It's a church problem. Truth is—it has *always* been a church problem."[102]

Over the last five years, it has become increasingly common to hear youth workers talk about the importance of partnering with parents for discipleship of teenagers. In some ways, this is not new because it has always been a stated-goal, but it has rarely been an actual priority. Parents have often been viewed as opponents and with suspicion. But now, it is

---

[102]Wayne Rice, *Reinventing Youth Ministry (Again): From Bells and Whistles to Flesh and Blood* (Downers Grove, IL: Intervarsity Press, 2010), 24 & 144.

becoming apparent that a new era is dawning where youth ministry is more integrated with the church and more invested in parents.

Recently, the most rapidly growing conferences for youth workers have been the Orange Conference and the D6 Conference while Youth Specialties conferences have struggled to retain momentum.[103] It would be difficult to find a youth ministry conference that does not emphasize ministry to parents. The Rooted Conference reflects this trend as a good example as a conference for youth workers *and* parents with a specific track of workshops for youth workers and another for parents.

Bookshelves of resources are now published every year as handbooks, curricula, and ministry philosophy for a more parent-oriented and church-integrated model. It would be foolish to say there has not been a biblical argument for this new emphasis, but there have been very few books singularly committed to developing a biblical theology for the new era of youth ministry. Every influencer in this new era of youth ministry seems to be prioritizing intergenerational ministry and incorporating students in the life of the church-at-large.

From Christian Endeavor, to Young Life, to Youth for Christ, youth workers have consistently been among the most culturally-aware ministers of their generation. Whether one considers fashion or music styles or sexual norms, cultural change increasingly begins in youth culture. Youth culture has become a petri dish for marketers and ideologues to test their new products before introducing them into the broader society. For these reasons, the next era of youth workers, parents, and pastors will need to come together in true collaboration for the sake of the emerging generation. Understanding the history of modern youth ministry is not fodder for pointing a blaming finger on others, but a

---

[103]The National Youth Worker's Convention has been relaunched under new leadership and seems positioned to rebound. The drop from four yearly large-scale conferences to only one demonstrates increased competition from other conferences and the diminishing influence of Youth Specialties.

way to learn from one another. At the same time, youth workers would be wise to consider not only the last two hundred years of ministry to teenagers, but the last two thousand years of gospel-centered ministry to adolescents.

Conclusion: What Youth Workers Can Learn From Church History

In order for catechesis to set a pattern for youth ministry today, it is necessary to remember youth workers today do not need to be trail blazers who carve their own path. The Church has been faithful to the biblical commands to raise up the next generation, and while culture shifts and changes, there are patterns and core-commitments to be learned from those who have come before. Catechesis does not depend upon rigid commitment to written catechisms; it rests upon a faithful commitment to evangelism and discipleship where the catechist (or, youth minister, in this case) methodically and intentionally teaches Christian doctrine and Christian living to those who have expressed the desire to learn. Catechisms may serve as a faithful tool that inform and benefit modern youth workers and parents, even if they are not used as the focal-point of the process.[104]

A faithful youth pastor desires to see both churched and unchurched students come to a saving knowledge of Christ while also equipping "church kids" to understand and grow in the gospel they have heard from childhood. Youth ministry desires to see students become members of the Church through faith and members of a local church by participation in God's ongoing work in that particular community. To this end, a church must resist seeing youth ministry as primarily a place in church to keep students from being bored. At the

---

[104]For a thoughtful exploration of building a youth ministry around catechesis, see: Brian Cosbey, *Giving Up Gimmicks: Reclaiming Youth Ministry from an Entertainment Culture* (Phillipsburg, NJ: P&R Publishing, 2012).

same time, youth workers can easily be so drawn to evangelism that discipleship gets overlooked. The Early Church sets a faithful example of the local church's public witness through counter-cultural Christ-likeness and through having a well-organized discipleship plan for new converts. The church ought to uphold youth ministry as an important and legitimate opportunity to see students who are far from God drawn near and set into relationship with godly adults who will disciple him or her while also seeking to develop a similar relationship with the student's family.

Youth ministry would be wise to consult the catechetical practices of the Church regarding what content was taught at each stage along the journey. Many youth group meetings are well-positioned to provide ministry to *Inquirers* and *Catechumens*, and integration in the church ought to be a priority with these students as they progress closer to baptism and toward Christian maturity. As the teacher in a youth group setting prepares, he or she ought to consider the audience, keeping the *Inquirers* and *Catechumens* in mind while preparing to tell the broad story of the gospel. As the gospel is proclaimed to students, they should be encouraged to consider baptism and involvement in the church body beyond the youth ministry. As students grow in Christ and in their understanding of the family of God (the Church), the youth workers would be wise to provide classes and other structured opportunities for the teenagers to receive more direct and intentional instruction from other adults in the church. As students continue to grow in maturity, they are to be encouraged to put their spiritual gifts to work within the local church, not only in the youth ministry. In a time when the youth ministry market is flooded with curricula promising new and creative Bible lessons, perhaps more churches should return to time-tested historic catechisms as the foundation for discipleship. The overall structure of the Early Church's catechesis can serve as a helpful guide in youth ministry. The objective of catechesis is not great theological knowledge as an end-in-itself, but a biblically informed love for God and for others.

Modern youth ministry is still transitioning into a new era where parents and the church are more than stated-values, they are actual priorities. If this observation about the future of youth ministry is accurate, there will be much to gain by rediscovering the Church's practice of catechesis. Previous generations of modern youth workers should not be condemned for leading ministry to youth astray, but it must be acknowledged that many of the practices developed over the last two hundred years are in stark contrast with the Church's legacy of ministry to the emerging generation. Rather than building on entertainment in order to get students to show up, church-based and parachurch youth workers need to first and foremost build upon the gospel. There is a significant difference between ministry philosophies that begin with getting youth to show up and then try to figure out how to communicate the gospel, and those approaches who begin with the gospel and then discern how to give that invitation to teenagers. Additionally, a renewal of catechesis would also serve in the same way it did in the Reformation: it would catechize the parents as they catechize their children. Catechesis begins in the Word of God and moves outward to the person being catechized through a relationship with the catechist that will be most fruitful. This is how the Church has always built disciples until recent generations. Perhaps it is time to realize there is more to learn from Church History than expected.

Matthew Henry reflects on the importance of both parents and the church when he writes, "Now those two methods of instruction, both by parents in their families, and by ministers in more public assemblies, are necessary, and do mutually assist each other, and neither will excuse the want of the other."[105] Catechetical ministry to youth must

---

[105]Henry, *Family Religion*, 66.

not be regarded as the task of either the family or the church—it must be the commitment of both, for both parents and ministers will be held accountable to God for how they fulfilled their God-given duties. The example of Richard Baxter's ministry in Kidderminster is not an example that is either repeatable nor the universal ideal for what a church should do—but it is a demonstration of the culture-shaping potential of catechesis and family-discipleship. If a church desires to see lasting generational change there must be an emphasis on discipling parents so they can disciple their children. In the midst of today's spiritual crises in America where both adults and youth are growing less committed to biblical Christianity, the Church ought to remember its disciple-making mission. The nature of catechesis provides structure for both doctrinal and ethical instruction in the context of an ongoing relationship. A catechetical structure of ministry faithfully reflects the Apostle Paul's words in 1 Thessalonians 2:8 when he writes, "*Because we loved you so much, we were delighted to share with you not only the gospel of God but our lives as well*" (NIV).

Chapter 5

Ecclesiology and Youth Ministry

Youth ministry is for adolescence. The family is for life. The Church is for eternity. Therefore, a biblical theology of youth ministry must be primarily anchored in the Church, for this is the true family to which all Christians eternally belong. The family's significance is so profound because it is a living metaphor for the Church. Finally, youth ministry is poised as a bridge to connect the Church and the family in their efforts to co-evangelize and co-disciple the next generation.

A practical theology of the Church must include not only an understanding of the Bible's teaching about the Church, it must also recognize that ministry does not happen in a culture-less vacuum. After all, Jesus spoke in Aramaic and the Bible was written in Koine Greek, both of which represent the languages of the common person on the receiving-end of the biblical message. Because of the ministry of the Church takes place in culture, this chapter begins with an exploration of today's generation of teenagers before exploring a biblical theology of the Church.

Much of the content of this book is presented objectively and exegetically in order to anchor today's ministry in the unchanging authority of God's Word. Like good missionaries, Christian parents and church leaders must acknowledge that culture plays a formative role in children as they navigate adolescence, and culture cannot simply be avoided through homeschool or private schooling. Additionally, culture is not inherently evil or sinful and should not be viewed as something to be cleansed from the Christian's life. Culture is to humanity what water is to a fish. Awareness of generational trends is not capitulation toward a godless culture. Instead, love is what fuels parents and ministers to understand what is happening in youth culture, so the gospel would be effectively and compellingly proclaimed and applied. The following summary is provided based of the most current research at the time of this book's writing.

Who is GenZ?

Research on the current generation of teenagers is so new, there is a debate regarding what they should be called. The leading candidates proposed are Gen Z, Generation Z, iGen, and Digital Natives. Jean Twenge, who makes a compelling argument for the name *iGen*, points out that no generation that was dependent on the previous generation has ever stuck. Generation X rejected the label *Baby Busters* and Millennials rejected *Generation Y*, because both names weren't descriptive of their generation.[106] While the name iGen seems most appropriate, *GenZ* simply remains the most common name to date and will be the preferred label in this book.

Twenge issues a harrowing warning: "With iGen'ers still emerging into adulthood, their religious orientation is a harbinger of what the United States will look like in the coming decades—whether that's shuttered churches or a new revival of American religion.... A full third

---

[106]Jean M. Twenge, *iGen: Why Today's Super-Connected Kids Are Growing Up Less Rebellious, More Tolerant, Less Happy—and Completely Unprepared for Adulthood* (New York, NY: Atria Books, 2017), 7.

of young adults do not affiliate with any organized religion."[107] Those who are religiously devout face increasing scrutiny, as it is more socially acceptable to be either nonreligious or religiously ambivalent than it is to be convinced that one particular faith has "the truth." The older generations in the church often assume that young people will "come back" when they start having children of their own, but this simply is not reflected in sociological data.[108]

Among the most notable shifts within GenZ is the emphasis on tolerance and diversity. With the increasing attention sexuality has received in recent times, some may have grown weary of these conversations but they are very much needed. Sexuality remains at the forefront of generational distinctives for GenZ: "1/8 describes their sexual orientation as something other than heterosexual" and "7/10 agree that it is acceptable to be born one gender and feel like another."[109] It is significant that 77% of "engaged Christians" agreed that homosexuality "is morally wrong," but this figure drops to 24% and 13% among "churched Christians" and "unchurched Christians." These numbers portray a rift among professing Christians when it comes to views on sexuality. This emphasis on tolerance extends beyond sexuality to the degree that 24% of GenZ agrees that "What is morally right and wrong changes over time based on society,"[110] and, further, 21% agree "What is morally right or wrong depends on what an individual believes."[111] Rather than toning down conversations about sexual identity, the Church will need to learn how to better grapple with GenZ's views on sexuality in order to graciously and discerningly communicate a biblical sexual

---

[107]Ibid, 120-121.

[108]Ibid, 124-5. She writes, "Millennials have not been returning to religious institutions during their twenties and thirties, making it unlikely that iGen'ers will, either."

[109]Ibid, 40.

[110]Barna Group, *Gen Z: the Culture, Beliefs and Motivations Shaping the Next Generation* (Ventura, CA: Barna Group, 2018), 55.

[111]Ibid.

ethic. Shouting about absolute truth and "saying it like it is" will only prove to GenZ that conservative Christians are intolerant bigots.

The phrase "spiritual but not religious" may reflect the attitude among Millennials who retained much of their religious upbringing without remaining committed to any particular organized religion, but this phrase is not emblematic of GenZ. Instead, they are increasingly neither spiritual nor religious. Beginning in 2006, studies began to reflect a disbelief in the afterlife or anything spiritual.[112] Research from the Barna Research Group and Impact 360 also reflects this atheistic turn: "Teens 13 to 18 years old are twice as likely as adults to say they are atheist (13% vs. 6%). Only three in five identify as Christian, compared to two-thirds of adults (59% vs 68%)."[113] American culture has been labeled "post-Christian" for some time, but this is especially pronounced among teenagers, of whom, only 4% hold a biblical worldview.[114] It may seem that nominal Christians have merely become honest about their *actual* religious beliefs rather that conforming to cultural pressure to appear Christian. James Emery White explains that what is most concerning is the loss of a "squishy middle."[115] This is the group of people who have historically been the most receptive to the Church's evangelistic efforts. Without this group, evangelism will grow increasingly difficult and discipleship will look even more counter-cultural. No longer are Christians evangelizing men and women who are warm towards the church but remain uncommitted to Christ; instead, they are evangelizing a truly post-Christian people who have deliberately chosen to not be affiliated with the Church. As this secular drift continues, the trick-

---

[112]Twenge, *iGen*, 127-129.

[113]Barna Group, *Gen Z*, 14.

[114]Ibid, 24-25. The following was also reported as the percentage of each generational population with a biblical worldview: 10% of Baby Boomers, 7% of Gen X, 6% of Millennials.

[115]James Emery White, *Meet Generation Z: Understanding and Reaching the new Post-Christian World* (Grand Rapids, MI: Baker Books, 2017), 32.

le-down effect on teenagers will grow increasingly prominent, as will the need for youth workers who are equipped as both disciple-makers and evangelists.

While the future of the Church is secure ("the gates of Hell will not prevail against it," Matthew 16:18), the local church will look very different in the coming decades because of these shifts. It is highly likely that the role of the Church will move further toward the fringe of cultural influence, church size will shrink (along with staff and budgets), and churches will need to become more focused in their ministry to their community. It is not acceptable to discount the above statistics as arguments that are anchored in culture rather than in Scripture—this is a portrait of a generation God has called the Church to minister unto. The remainder of this chapter emphasizes the Church's call to evangelize and disciple all people, and that must include the children and teenagers. In this post-Christian culture, the overwhelming majority of committed Christians have never been intentionally discipled or mentored. As in the days of the Reformation, calling parents to family discipleship only adds a burden around their neck, because they do not know how to carry out that calling. The church must not only call parents to family discipleship, but practically equip and empower them for the task.

Finally, Twenge makes an astute observation, "In a society where young people hear 'If it feels good, do it' and 'Believe in yourself,' religion seems almost countercultural."[116] The Church exists to spread the greatest message: that God saves sinners through Jesus, and makes them a family through the indwelling Holy Spirit. When churches are convinced of the need for intergenerational ministry and family discipleship, they will do well to remember the many teenagers described above who are being raised in nonreligious households. Rather than

---

[116]Twenge, *iGen*, 138.

view family discipleship in the church as something that ostracizes teens from nonbelieving families, this commitment should enfold them into the church family as dearly loved members of the family of God.

Ecclesiology Shapes Youth Ministry

Pastoral ministry is inherently a theological pursuit. The daily work of ministry is an overflow of the pastor's theology. However, like the vegetarian who consistently eats hamburgers but refuses to admit he is not really a vegetarian, there are many pastors who refuse to admit when their *actual theology* does not match their *stated theology*.[117] The previous generation of youth workers has largely undervalued ecclesiology in their theological foundations of youth ministry, and consequently, in their practice. If youth workers continue to overlook the importance of ecclesiology in youth ministry, it will bring significant long-term harm to the local church as a rising generation continues to misunderstand their identity as members in Christ's Church. In an effort to build youth ministry on a theological foundation that aligns both stated and actual theological convictions, this chapter presents ecclesiology with an eye toward practical implications for ministry to teenagers.

The Nature of the Church

The mission of the Church flows out from understanding the nature of the Church. Millard Erickson's *Christian Theology* provides a helpful threefold description[118] that provides a Trinitarian context for

---

[117]For example, while most evangelical pastors agree the Bible is the inspired, authoritative Word of God they give other books and resources to non-Christians because the Bible is too confusing. If the Bible is the Word of God and Christians withhold it from those who need to hear from God, there is a disconnect between that person's stated and actual theology of what the Bible is. This does not discount the value of other resources for non-Christians, but merely highlights the confidence that should exist in the Holy Spirit to work through the Bible He inspired.

[118]Millard J. Erickson, *Christian Theology*, 2nd ed. (Grand Rapids, MI: Baker, 1998), 1045-51.

understanding the relationship between ecclesiology and ministry to students. Before addressing the nature of the Church, however, it is important to keep in mind both the distinction and overlap between the Church and the local church.[119]

Dual-Nature of the Church

The Church is both a universal fellowship of Christians, and an organized gathering of Christians who worship God by prioritizing the preaching of Scripture, the administration of the ordinances, and the exercise of church discipline.[120] It has become increasingly common for Christians to identify as members of the Church without embracing their role as members of a local church. The most obvious biblical passage addressing this weak ecclesiology is found in Hebrews 10:24-25, "*And let us consider how to stir up one another to love and good works, not neglecting to meet together, as is the habit of some, but encouraging one another, and all the more as you see the Day drawing near.*" First John 1:7, which was written to a church enduring division and strife, makes it clear that "*walking in the light*" not only produces unity with Christ, but also produces "*fellowship with one another.*" Participation in a church without any commitment to that body of believers would have been unthinkable to the early Christians. Furthermore, Paul's ministry throughout the book of Acts demonstrates the importance of an organized group of Christians who are committed to worship, teaching, and church discipline in order to fulfill the Great Commission. The New Testament vision is for the local church to reflect the unity of the Universal Church. This is why the Creeds of the Church have been so influential throughout

---

[119]Two recommended books for further study are Edmund P. Clowney, *The Church* (Downer's Grove, IL: IVP, 1995) and Mark Dever, *The Church: The Gospel Made Visible* (Nashville, TN: B&H Publishing, 2012)

[120]This distinction will be carried throughout this book by "Church" referring to the Universal Church while "church" refers more specifically to the local church.

church history, because despite all the differences that can divide the churches, they are united by the Creeds.

The distinction between the Church and the church is important for youth ministry because while much emphasis is given to evangelism and helping students become Christians (members of the Church), until recent years, there has been little emphasis on students' identity as contributors in the local church. There are many churches whose children and teenagers have separate programs for them during the church's gathered worship service, leading students to never need to join the adults in worship until they graduate high school. In these cases, it is worth asking whether or not these students actually attend church at all. Ministries who emphasize the gospel's invitation into the Church without working to include students in the life of the church are simply unbiblical and narrow-sighted. Both parachurch and church-based ministries are called to seek avenues to incorporate students into the local church as much as possible so students would thrive as life-long disciples. This is probably easier for small churches than it is for larger churches and for parachurch ministries, but it is a necessary and biblical commitment that must be held and followed through upon.

The Church Is the People of God

Every Christian has been adopted into the people of God (Ephesians 1:4-5.). Throughout the Old Testament, Israel is referred to as the "people of God." Erickson distinguishes Israel and the Church as God's people this way, "In the Old Testament, [God] did not adopt as his own an existing nation, but actually *created* a people for himself.... In the New Testament, this concept of God's choosing a people is broadened to include both Jews and Gentiles within the church."[121] There are not two separate people of God, but an enfolding and a broadening of what was always meant by that designation. This is most clearly artic-

---

[121]Erickson, *Christian Theology*, 1045.

ulated in Romans 11:11-24 where Paul emphasizes that Gentiles are wild branches who have become ingrafted into the olive tree of Israel. The Church is composed of both Jews and Gentiles as fulfillment of the LORD's promise to Abraham, *"In you all the families of the earth shall be blessed"* (Genesis 12:3). In 2 Corinthians 6:16 the Apostle Paul says the Church is heir of the promise given to Israel.[122] Accordingly, 1 Peter 2:9-10 declares, *"But you are a chosen race, a royal priesthood, a holy nation, a people for his own possession, that you may proclaim the excellencies of him who called you out of darkness into his marvelous light. Once you were not a people, but now you are God's people; once you had not received mercy, but now you have received mercy."* God's people are no longer marked by circumcision, but "circumcision of the heart," which points to the righteousness of God that comes through faith in Jesus Christ (Romans 2:25-29, 3:21-26).

Christians are the people of God, and there is no age restriction mentioned. They are a holy people. And this is true whether or not the individual is a child who newly understands the gospel or a saint who is approaching his or her final days in old age. This is popularly referenced when people declare, "Teenagers aren't the church of tomorrow, they are the church of today." Even though children and teenagers are not typically eligible for official membership in the local church membership, it must be agreed upon there are no *junior members* in the Church. As Church members and as participants in the local church, the entire church shares a commitment to and affirmation of the vital importance of teenagers in the church-at-large. Some of the most spiritual mature people in the church should be serving in the children's and youth ministries. Practically speaking, this means students are not merely passed off to youth and children's ministry workers while the "big boys" minister to the adults. Instead, the entire church shares a commitment to nurture the faith of the next generation while seeking

---

[122]Ex. 6:7; Lev. 26:12; Jer. 7:23, 11:4, 30:22; Ezek. 36:28.

opportunities to involve them into the rhythms of the church. Especially considering the above statistics regarding GenZ's religious beliefs, the local church should be committed to seeing this generation transformed by the power of the gospel. When a church is only interested in ministering to the children and teenagers of their own families, they have lost sight of the Church's identity as the people of God, for Church membership is not transferred genetically but through the transformational power of the gospel.

The Church Is the Body of Christ

Ephesians 1:22-23 addresses Christ's relationship with the Church this way, "*And God placed all things under his feet and appointed him to be head over everything for the church, which is his body, the fullness of him who fills everything in every way*" (NIV). Colossians 1:18 repeats nearly the exact same statement, "*And he is the head of the body, the church*" (NIV). Paul's use of the Greek κεφαλή (*kefalē*, meaning "head") as a description of Jesus' relationship to the Church in Ephesians 1:22, 5:23, and Colossians 1:18 points to the supremacy of Christ in the Church. As the body of Christ, the Church is not free to do whatever she likes, but must submit to Christ. Christians are under the gospel rather than the law—they are people marked by grace. Accordingly, ministry in the church is to be Christ-centered in every area.

This understanding of the Church as the body of Christ is also carried forth in 1 Corinthians 12 and Romans 12:4-8 where Paul applies this same "body" metaphor to the local church. Reflecting the dual-nature of the Church, Christ is the Lord and head while the people serve a significant role as members within the church. Each Christian is given a spiritual gift in order to exercise ministry in the body of Christ, for the benefit of both the local church and the world. Christians depend on one another and are deeply connected because a local church must not be content to simply rely on a mouth that preaches or a hand that serves; it must embrace the gifts of the many members in order to function as a whole body. Erickson explains, "While there is diversity of gifts, there is not to be division within the body. Some of these gifts are more conspicuous than others, but they are not therefore more important."[123] When each member is serving the head of the Church with their individual gifts, the members are united together through the bond of Christian fellowship as the body of Christ works in harmony. First Timothy 4:12 famously encourages young Christians, "*Let no one despise you for your youth, but set the believers an example in speech, in conduct, in love, in faith, in purity.*"

Although the former generations have often treated children and teenagers as those who should be "seen but not heard," there has been a growing number of churches who are incorporating teenagers into the regular rhythms of their church's ministries.[124] This is an encouraging movement that beautifully captures the truth of the Church as the people of God and the body of Christ—where teenagers are not viewed as "members in waiting," but as genuinely converted Christians who have a role to play in the body of Christ. What a beautiful expression of the body of Christ it would be for teenagers to be paired with mature Christians in various ministry roles! This would provide much-needed mentoring and discipleship for the teenager while also empowering them for a lifetime of ongoing ministry in the church. It is good for teenagers to serve in the children's ministry and in their own youth ministry, but it would greatly benefit youth workers to create inroads to ministry opportunities beyond the youth ministry where teenagers can serve as members in the body of Christ.

---

[123]Erickson, *Christian Theology*, 1048.

[124]Kara Eckmann Powell, *Growing Young: Six Essential Strategies to Help Young People Discover and Love Your Church* (Grand Rapids, MI: Baker Books, 2016).

The Church Is the Temple of the Holy Spirit

Because of Pentecost, Christians are both individually and corporately marked by the indwelling of the Holy Spirit. Previously, the Holy Spirit empowered Old Testament saints for particular tasks and lived among the people (in the Holy of Holies) but not in the people. Pentecost (Acts 2:1-4) marks significant change of action: the third Person of the Holy Trinity now indwells Christians, making them into a living temple. The Apostle Paul urges the churches toward holiness by asking, "*Do you not know that you are God's temple and that God's Spirit dwells in you?*" (1 Corinthians 3:16) and "*Or do you not know that your body is a temple of the Holy Spirit within you, whom you have from God?*" (1 Corinthians 6:19). Additionally, Jesus promised His disciples that He would send them "another helper" *(παράκλητος, or paraclete)* who, "*dwells with you and will be in you*" (John 14:17).

Throughout the New Testament, the Church is built and established through the proclamation of the gospel and the miraculous work of the Holy Spirit. The Holy Spirit was not only necessary for miraculous healings in the early church, but for the very formation of the Church as the people of God, the body of Christ, and as a living temple where the Holy Spirit resides (Ephesians 2:8-9.). He does not merely empower the Church, He is also the one who makes the Church holy. As Erickson writes, "…just as the temple was a holy and sacred place under the old covenant because God dwelt in it, so also are believers sanctified under the new covenant because they are the temple of the Holy Spirit."[125] Without the ongoing work of the Holy Spirit, the Church would fail to grow in holiness and Christians would rely on their own power and wisdom in their ministry to one another and the world.

Among the 90 New Testament references where "Holy Spirit" and "you" appear in the same verse, the only times the Holy Spirit is given

---

[125]Erickson, *Christian Theology*, 1051.

to a singular "you" is Mary at the Annunciation (Luke 1:35) and the Apostle Paul at his conversion with Ananias (Acts 9:17). Every reference in the New Testament to "you" being filled or indwelled with the Holy Spirit, except for the Apostle Paul's conversion in Acts 9:17, is plural not singular. In the midst of today's rampant individualism where many seek private spirituality apart from public expressions of faith, the Scriptures consistently emphasize that the Church is the Temple of the Holy Spirit. Christians have been united with Christ (John 17:20-26; Romans 6:5; Galatians 3:7), not merely as individuals, but as one body with many members. It is biblical and good to affirm that the Holy Spirit lives within each individual Christian, but this is always taught within context of Christians together as the people of God, the body of Christ, and the temple of the Holy Spirit.

Whether the youth worker in question is a parent, a parachurch worker, or a church-based pastor, there is a temptation to forget the practical implications of ecclesiology for teenagers. First, students are not simply called alone, but into community. They are invited into a diverse and intergenerational fellowship of Christians who are quite different from one another. Where technology promises to form diverse friendships and community but often leads to heightened rates of depression and loneliness,[126] the Church is the communion of saints. Second, students share in the Church's mission to make disciples of all peoples. Teenagers belong in the church and are members of the Church through saving faith in Jesus Christ, even if they are not yet church members. As members of the body of Christ they too have spiritual gifts to develop and utilize in fulfilling the mission of the Church. When youth ministries embrace the significance of participation in the

---

[126]Brian A. Primack, et al. "Social Media Use and Perceived Social Isolation Among Young Adults in the U.S.," *American Journal of Preventive Medicine*, Volume 53 , Issue 1, 1-8.

local church there will finally be agreement between stated their ecclesiology and actual ecclesiology.

The Mission of the Church: The Great Commission

In an effort to correct the contemporary trend where parents and church leaders completely entrust ministry to teenagers to the youth ministry, some have so emphasized the parents' role they functionally eliminated the church's mandate to evangelize and disciple the next generation. It is good and right to call parents to family discipleship, but this emphasis must not neglect the large percentage of children and youth who are not being raised by Christian parents. It is vital to consider the Church's role in evangelism and discipleship with those whose parents will not be partners (and will sometimes even be opposed to their children's newfound relationship with Christ). Therefore, it is fitting to revisit the Great Commission as Scripture's clearest description of the mission of the Church.

In Matthew 28:18-20, Jesus gave the following charge to His disciples and to the Church, *"All authority in heaven and on earth has been given to me. Go therefore and make disciples of all nations, baptizing them in the name of the Father and of the Son and of the Holy Spirit, teaching them to observe all that I have commanded you. And behold, I am with you always, to the end of the age."* The fundamental mission of the Church is rooted in the message of the gospel. Without the gospel, there is no Church. The Great Commission can be explained as one command, two promises, and three pathways.

The one command is the only verb in the Great Commission, μαθητεύσατε (*mathēteuō*), translated as "make disciples." The other words that look like verbs ("go," "baptizing," and "teaching") are active participles that function as subordinate verbs meant to explain or clarify the verb ("make disciples") they depend upon. Jesus commands His disciples to fix their eyes on one singular goal: to make disciples. The mission of the Church isn't accomplished in a day. Instead, the verb form (present active indicative) reflects an ongoing command that is to be carried out repeatedly. In the midst of everything else a church does, she must prioritize disciple-making in all things or risk drifting from the heartbeat of the Great Commission.

Jesus gives His disciples two promises the Church is built upon: *"all authority in heaven and earth have been given to me"* and *"I will be with you always, to the end of the age."* This may be the most neglected and overlooked part of the Great Commission. The disciples' success in disciple-making comes from Jesus' authority and presence with them, not upon their ability. The gospel is a proclamation that Jesus has received all authority in heaven and earth, and that He has done everything necessary for the salvation and new life of all who follow Him. Not only does He have this authority, but He has empowered Christians by the indwelling Holy Spirit to live as His ambassadors to a lost world. The mission of the Church, whether directed toward students, parents, singles, or senior citizens, is dependent upon Jesus' authority and His presence among His people.

Meanwhile Jesus does indeed give His disciples three pathways to walk upon. There are three present active participles: πορευθέντες (*poreuthentes*) "go," βαπτίζοντες (*baptizontes*) "baptizing," and διδάσκοντες (*didaskontes*) "teaching." These are the pathways by which the disciple-making mission is accomplished. While it is popularly said that Jesus never dictated methods, only mission—the Great Commission disagrees. It is true Jesus never explicitly states which exact location to go to, how many liters of water are required for baptism, or how long the ideal sermon should last. This does not mean He was silent regarding the ministry priorities of the church. This is important because it clarifies disciples as the primary mission, and it is accomplished through going, baptizing, and teaching. Without each of those three pathways, the

Great Commission is pursued in ways disobedient to Jesus' instruction. Thus, building a "come and see" church that seeks to fuse evangelism with entertainment is ironically opposed to the Great Commission. Instead, the church must be a people who goes to all people groups (teenagers included), in order to see them converted and baptized as members of Christ's Church, and then taught about the way, the truth, and the life. Overall, youth ministries tend to be strong on the "going" pathway, give attention to the "baptizing" pathway because it celebrates those who are baby Christians, but "teaching" has fallen on hard times and is increasingly viewed with suspicion as overly authoritative. Teenagers simply must be taught sound doctrine. Bible study should not be shrouded with a "been there, done that" skepticism, but with a firm conviction that this is how Jesus instructed His disciples to build the Church. There are many different teaching styles, and there is freedom in youth ministry to employ those, but it is central to maintain a regular time when students are instructed according to the Word of God.

Practical Considerations for Ecclesiology and Youth Ministry

A Call for Intergenerational Ministry

Intergenerational discipleship must become an actual value rather than an aspirational value in order to equip believers to fulfill their created purpose of worshiping God and working in a way that reflects God's sovereignty over all creation. Choosing to be faithful in discipleship to the children and youth of church members does not exempt the church from ministry to unchurched children and youth. Neither does prioritizing evangelism of the unchurched minimize the value of ministry to "church kids." Too often, evangelism and discipleship have been separated as if they are mutually-exclusive. Instead, the church is called to make disciples of both by ministering to each group according to their backgrounds.

When a church is committed to the Great Commission, that church will prioritize discipleship in everything they do, including making disciples out of those who were previously opposed to Christ. Youth ministry is a disciple-making ministry where the gospel is proclaimed and applied to the real-life situations teenagers find themselves facing while they discover their identity as a member of Christ's Church; not simply a church-based club for teenagers to build healthy friendships and stay out of trouble. This is the biblical expectation for youth ministry and must be insisted upon by church leaders, parachurch leaders, and parents. Those who are mature ought to intentionally pursue opportunities to disciple those who are younger, and those who are younger must be teachable and humble enough to learn.

Teenagers are not simply "future church members" who are treated only according to their future potential to contribute. Dave Wright explains, "In order to integrate students into all aspects of the life of a congregation, the members must see the capabilities of youth. They must not be seen as the church of tomorrow but brought into the life of the church *today*."[127] Thankfully, this is a growing concern among ministry leaders—most notably through efforts like the *D6 Conference* [128]and the "Growing Young"[129] campaign of the *Fuller Youth Institute*. The next era of youth ministry must recover the integral role of the church in developing lifelong disciples.

---

[127]Dave Wright, "Gathering God's People: Generational Integration in Youth Ministry," in *Gospel-Centered Youth Ministry: A Practical Guide,* Cameron Cole & Jon Nielson, eds. (Wheaton, IL: Crossway, 2016), 111.

[128]Learn more at: www.d6family.com/d6conference.

[129]Kara Powell, *Growing Young: Six Essential Strategies to Help Young People Discover and Love Your Church* (Grand Rapids, MI: Baker, 2016).

Church Membership and Teenagers

Church membership is not simply a matter of interviews before an elder or deacon board and signing a church's statement of faith. Church membership must *begin* with adoption into the Church through the confession of Jesus Christ as Lord (Romans 10:9). The church member is someone who has been adopted into the family of God, the body of Christ, and temple of the Holy Spirit by grace through faith, not by works. Certainly, there is more to church membership than this, such as affirmation of that church's particular doctrines in secondary matters and agreement with the church's ministry philosophy; but church membership is, at its core, a recognition of Church membership.

When teenagers have been baptized after a credible confession of faith and demonstrating the fruit of repentance, encouraging church membership seems like a wise avenue to express, "You are a real Christian. You are a member of the family of God. You belong here." On the other hand, minimizing church members often conveys, "Church membership isn't important because you can keep attending here without becoming a member." It is rare to find churches who encourage teenagers to become official members of the church, and many who do include statements such as, "Only members over the age 18 are voting members." Church leaders who read this book certainly need to abide by their church constitution and bylaws, but it might prove to be a constructive conversation to raise the question about church membership for teenagers among the senior leadership of the church.

Conclusion: Bringing Ecclesiology to Youth Ministry

The Church's mission is centered around the gospel, and youth workers should remember, "The church not only *says* God's mission, it *does* God's mission because it embodies the very reality of God. The church by its very existence makes the reality of God present."[130] If the Church and parents are mutually committed to seeing their children come to saving faith and grow into maturity in Christ, mere "salvation" cannot be the goal. Unfortunately, it has become common to minister to teenagers in a way that is entirely disconnected from the local church. Parachurch ministries, in an effort to avoid appearances of favoritism, avoid "endorsing" one particular local church in their community while others build such high expectations for students (and leaders) in their program it is practically impossible to be a committed church member while also participating in the parachurch ministry. And yet this is not a parachurch-only problem. Many churches even encourage their youth ministries to hold a "youth service" on Sunday mornings while the adults are gathered for worship in the sanctuary. Church-based youth ministries often build up their ministries in such a way they are functionally a parachurch ministry that is funded by and hosted by the local church, but there is very little overlap between the youth ministry and the ministries of the church. Churchless youth ministry has resulted in a generation who has largely concluded the church is simply "present," but certainly is not worthy of devotion or meaningful sacrifice.[131]

In considering the mission of the Church, it is essential to remember that, "As the body of Christ, the church is the extension of [Christ's] ministry."[132] The importance of the Church and the church are difficult to overstate. Jesus promised the very gates of hell would not prevail against the Church (Matthew 16:18). It is both unbiblical and foolish to divorce youth ministry from the Bride of Christ. The Church, not Israel and not the family, is the central means through which God has

---

[130]Robert Webber, *Ancient-Future Evangelism: Making Your Church a Faith-Forming Community*, 2nd printing (Grand Rapids, MI: Baker, 2004), 74.

[131]David Kinnaman with Aly Hawkins, *You Lost Me: Why Young Christians Are Leaving Church—and Rethinking Faith* (Grand Rapids, MI: Baker Books, 2011), 113-129.

[132]Erickson, *Christian Theology*, 1049.

chosen to continue His work until Christ's return. May these biblical and theological foundations for youth ministry serve as reminders to be a bridge, connecting the church and home while building lifelong disciples whose faith is firmly planted in the Church.

Chapter 6

The Family and Youth Ministry

The American family is in crisis. This much is clear and undeniable. More children than ever are being raised in households without both biological parents due to either divorce or parents who never got married in the first place. Ironically, marriage has become the battleground for LGBTQ rights, even as it is repudiated as old fashioned and unnecessary by a generation of heterosexual couples who are cohabitating. Biblical teaching on the family as a husband and wife in lifelong commitment to one another and to their children is increasingly counter-cultural, and has even been called bigoted and oppressive.

A wise Christian response to this crisis is both firm and humble. Firm because God has spoken, and efforts to improve upon His design for humanity will only be met with greater brokenness and judgment. Humble because these are sensitive days when a previous generation's "culture war" has left the younger generation with the impression that Christians are cultural bullies who manipulate others to get their own way. As churches, parents, and youth workers collaborate to minister to the next generation, it will become extremely important to lay a biblical foundation for what the family is. Understanding the biblical teaching on the family will provide students with a better view of God's good design while also nurturing healthier families who take the calling of family discipleship seriously (rather than being content to off-load discipleship to the church and youth ministry). The mission and purpose of the family is anchored in creation. Therefore, it is unthinkable to separate the nature of the family from its purpose.

The Biblical Vision for the Family

Creation and Origin of the Family

In considering the origin and nature of the family, it makes sense to begin in context of Adam and Eve's created purpose. Adam's task is explained in Genesis 2:15 as, "*The LORD God took the man and put him in the garden of Eden to work it and keep it.*" In this verse, the Hebrew word לְעָבְדָהּ (*leʿobdah*) is translated as "work" in most major Bible translations, yet throughout the remainder of the Old Testament it is translated as "serve."[133] With this in mind, the root word עֶבֶד (*ʿebed*) carries the weight of religious service and worship, not mere gardening. Thus, the language used in Genesis 2:15 reflects that of faithful worshipers, serving their God by working the garden. Tending the garden was sacred work. It is also important to recognize that work is not a result of the fall, but is a fundamental aspect of being human. Adam's calling to worship and to work ought to be seen as complementary duties, which remain a core component of human calling. The separation of "sacred" and "secular" work is entirely unbiblical and contrary to the sacred work in Genesis 2:15. It must also be recognized that this calling is not simply restricted to Eden, but remained even after the fall, though Adam continues to work the land in the midst of thorns and painful toil.[134]

---

[133]See: Deut. 11:13, 28:14; Josh. 22:5; Judg. 2:19; Jer. 11:10, 13:10, 25:6, 27:6, 35:15; Zeph. 3:9.
[134]Gen. 3:17-19.

Likewise, Eve was given as Adam's "helper" to fulfill this holy purpose for humanity. The word translated as "helper," the Hebrew עֵזֶר (*ēzer*), is used consistently in reference to reinforcements who are sent in to strengthen an ally during battle.[135] Eve is not given as Adam's wife simply to bear children and to "help" in menial or peripheral tasks. Instead, she is described as a helper who will strengthen Adam in order to victoriously fulfill his duty to worship God and to work the garden. When God created Eve out of Adam's rib in Genesis 2:21-24, He was creating more than gender. He created the family, the first human institution. Whereas the days of creation were consistently met with the refrain, "and it was good," Adam's loneliness (לְבַדּוֹ lᵉbaddô) in Genesis 2:18 marks the first time God declares something "not good." God's solution to Adam's isolation was the creation of marriage and family through Eve. Together, they carried out the calling of Genesis 2:15, to serve in the garden and to keep it.

Adam and Eve were placed in a garden: a place where things grow. From there, human culture has grown and expanded. Their calling to serve and keep the garden was a cultural mandate to build, grow, expand the world in which they were placed. Christians ought to have a similar worldview where every arena of life is an opportunity to express human creativity in a way that honors the command to work while beholding God's glory. The notion that religious workers have "sacred" jobs while those who work in banking or manual labor have "secular" jobs is entirely unbiblical. All arenas of life are opportunities to work and keep the garden. This is why Paul can say, "*And whatever you do, in word or deed, do everything in the name of the Lord Jesus, giving thanks to God the Father through him*" (Colossians 3:17).[136]

---

[135]Deut. 33:7; Ps. 89:20; Isa. 30:5; Dan. 11:34.

[136]Notably, Colossians 3:17 immediately precedes Paul's instructions for Christian households. It is entirely possibly he was thinking about Genesis 2:15, Adam and Eve's foundation, while he was instructing Christian households about their manner of conduct.

This transforms the way parents work both inside and outside the home, the way the family views education, the motive behind sports and playing together, and countless other facets of life. All these ought to be done in a way that recognizes God as the author and while exalting the creative goodness of God. The Christian home, therefore, is not simply a place of explicit worship flowing out from Scripture and prayer and singing; it is also an environment where everything in life is filtered and interpreted through a biblical worldview for the glory of God.[137]

Chapters 2 and 3 already laid the groundwork that the family is meant to be the primary disciple-maker of children. When Christian parents faithfully teach and model a biblical worldview of work as worship, children will flourish in their understanding of how to honor God in everything they do. The Christian family fulfills not only the calling given to all humanity as described above, but also the specific calling given to Christian disciples who live in a post-fall world by being a light to the world (Matthew 5:14-16). Accordingly, the family is a living parable of who God is and how He loves His children. When the Old Testament and New Testament teachings on the family are carried out, the mission of the family culminates in its unique ability to faithfully reflect the love of God to an unbelieving world. In so doing, the family also carries out the Great Commission.

"Family" in the Bible and the "Nuclear Family" Today

When reading about the family in Scripture, it is far too easy to impose today's assumptions about the family into the biblical teaching on family. Because of this unintended misreading of Scripture, it is important to consider the ways the modern family and family in the Bible are different. One surprising challenge is pinpointing a specific biblical

---

[137]For more on Christian worldview see: Albert M. Wolters, *Creation Regained: Biblical Basics for a Reformational Worldview*, 2nd ed. (Grand Rapids, MI: Wm. B. Eerdmans Publishing Company, 2005).

definition for "family." Exploring the various words used throughout the Old and New Testaments reveals a broad range of understanding about what the family is. Andreas J. Köstenberger explains,

> "The Old Testament features four major terms related to family: (1) 'am ('people'); (2) *sebet matteh* ('tribe'); (3) *mispahha* ('clan'); and (4) *bet 'ab* ('house of a father'). While 'am (people) typically has the nation of Israel as a referent and *sebet matteh* ('tribe') reflects the people's tribal structure as descendants of the twelve sons of Jacob, *misphaha* ('clan') usually designates a subgroup smaller than the tribe but larger than the family."[138]

The most direct Hebrew reference for the nuclear family is בֵּית אָב *bet 'ab* (house of a father). Stanley Porter agrees, stating, "There is no single term for 'family' in ancient Greek, especially in relation to what we think of today as a family, with a parent or two and 2.5 children."[139] Regarding the diverse language employed for the range of understanding family, the *Theological Wordbook of the Old Testament* concludes, "The word for the inhabitants of one house is usually בֵּית [*bet*] "house, household" or בֵּית אָב [*bet 'ab*]. מִשְׁפָּחָה [*mispahha*] most often refers to a circle of relatives with strong blood ties."[140] Even though בֵּית אָב (*bet 'ab*) is the clearest parallel with today's use of the word family, "The term most frequently translated 'family' is *mišpāḥâ*, which had a larger connotation than 'family.' It meant 'clan' and could be applied, e.g., to six hundred Danites from two villages (Judges 18:11)."[141]

---

[138]Andreas J. Köstenberger and David W. Jones, *God, Marriage, and Family: Rebuilding the Biblical Foundation*, 2nd ed. (Wheaton, IL: Crossway, 2010), 85-86.

[139]Stanley E. Porter, "Family in the Epistles," in *Family in the Bible: Exploring Customs, Culture, and Context*, ed. Richard S. Hess, M. Daniel, R. Carroll (Grand Rapids, MI: Baker Academic, 2003), 153.

[140]R. Laird Harris, Gleason L. Archer, Jr., Bruce Waltke, *Theological Wordbook of the Old Testament* (Chicago, IL: Moody Publishers, 2003), s.v. "חפש," n.p.

[141]L. Hunt, *International Standard Bible Encyclopedia (Revised)*, vol. 2, eds. George W. Bromiley, et al. (Grand Rapids, MI: Wm. B. Eerdmans,1979), 280.

This clan identity was not isolated to the Old Testament, but remained in New Testament families. Köstenberger writes, "In Jesus' day, the extended family lived together (e.g., Mark 1:30), typically sharing a three or four-room home."[142] Among the more common words employed in the New Testament for family is οἶκος (*oikos*), which literally means "house." Regarding the use of οἶκος, Porter notes that the New Testament writers would frequently use this term not simply in reference to a building, but in reference to the household, and sometimes even the extended family.[143] Whereas οἶκος reflects בַּיִת (*bet*), πατρια (*patria*) corresponds with אָב (*ab*), as demonstrated from Ephesians 3:15, "*from whom every family [πατρια] in heaven and on earth is named.*"

The reason these details are important is this: when the Bible describes the family as the primary spiritual influence of children, that calling is given to more than the child's father and mother. The biblical sense of family means family discipleship is a community project. It is obvious and clear that parents are to lead in raising their children in the fear of the Lord, but it unbiblical and narrow-sighted to ignore the community's role in ministry to the next generation. Where parents are negligent of their Christian calling to their family, it is good and right for those who are spiritually mature to offer gentle correction to the parents and to even fill the void for those children when necessary.

The "nuclear family" is a modern concept where the father and mother live with their children as an independent social unit separate from other extended family. The Oxford-English Dictionary dates the earliest usage of "Nuclear Family" to 1924, making the term (although not the reality) a fairly recent definition of the family. The stability of the nuclear family has been in decline throughout the past few decades due to increasing divorce rates and most recently with rising single-parent households where the parents were never married. This has caused

---

[142]Köstenberger & Jones, *God, Marriage, and Family*, 99.
[143]Porter, "Family in the Epistles," 152-3.

much turmoil in the American Church and has caused great alarm, for many good reasons. And yet, it must be acknowledged that the nuclear family was never the biblical ideal. The continuing breakdown of the American family is leading to an increasingly individualistic mindset where even family members are not welcome to offer counsel and wisdom regarding lifestyle and values. Fragmentation of the family has slowly renewed the lament of Adam's loneliness that marriage and family was intended to resolve. In some ways, the nuclear family is now experiencing the logical breakdown and isolation it began when it separated itself from the broader family and communal living experienced by previous generations.

Many modern Christian writers have been guilty of imposing their understanding of the modern nuclear family over the biblical meaning of "family." Western families have not only forsaken the biblical definition of family merely by redefining sexual norms, but also by separating themselves from their broader household. Consider how uncommon it is for adult siblings to live within driving distance and for grandchildren to actually grow up together with older relatives as a meaningful influence in their childhood. The solution is not to become Amish or to cast judgment on family members who need to move away. Instead, Christian families are wise to pursue opportunities to recover a sense of *mispahha* ('clan') by fostering a deep sense of family identity and belonging, even despite the geographical distance that may easily separate the clan.

The Family as a Mini-Church

Ancient Near Eastern cultures viewed the family as the central hub from which religion and spirituality flowed. The first century Jewish historian Josephus described the Jews' utmost priority as, "to educate our children well; and we think it to be the most necessary business of our whole life, to observe the laws that have been given us, and to keep those rules of piety that have been delivered down to us."[144] The *International Standard Bible Encyclopedia* further explains,

> "In Semitic society the family was much more than a mere social organism. One of its highly significant features was its function as a religious community. It was through the family that the cult of the household and the tribal deities was practiced and perpetuated. The father of the house, by virtue of being the family head, was the priest of the household. As such he was responsible for the religious life of his family; he maintained the family altar and he offered sacrifices to the family gods."[145]

Ancient cultures viewed parents as functional priests to their children, and their home was considered a sacred place where religion was taught. The religious community is pivotal for the next generation, but the family is undeniably the first and most important influence in the life of children.[146] The common practice where parents do their best to raise mature and responsible kids who become contributors to the culture while the church oversees their moral and spiritual development is contrary to biblical teaching for the family. Instead, every aspect of family life should be gospel-centered and reflect the mission given to Adam and Eve in Genesis 2:15.

George Whitefield taught that parents ought to read Scripture with their family, pray with their family, and catechize and instruct their family in the laws of God.[147] The first two of these exhortations may seem fairly obvious, while the third remains unclear to many families today.

---

[144]Josephus, *Against Apion in Complete Works*, trans. William Whiston (Grand Rapids, MI: Kregel Publications, 1960), 1:12.

[145]L. Hunt, 280.

[146]See: Vern L. Bengtson, *Families and Faith: How Religion Is Passed Down Across Generations*, (Oxford, UK: Oxford University Press, 2013).

[147]George Whitefield, *Selected Works of George Whitefield*, Accordance electronic ed. (Altamonte Springs, FL: OakTree Software, 1997), n.p.

Embracing the family as a mini-church does not mean there are hymns and sermons every day, though family discipleship ought to be a regular habit; but, it does mean Scripture and discussions about faith are common because the family was created for a God-centered purpose. Children are to be taught Scripture, not simply to gain knowledge, but that their hearts would be turned toward God in joyful obedience. Once again, Deuteronomy 6:4-9 is insightful regarding its exhortation for both formal ("teach them diligently") and informal ("talk about them when you sit in your house, and when you walk by the way...") instruction for children. In the midst of an abundance of books on Christian parenting, there seems to be a resurgence of books regarding this third calling of Christian parents that appears to remain a struggle. There also seems to be a resurgence in attention to family worship in recent years.[148] In a period where formal catechisms have fallen out of favor in Evangelicalism, the church must be careful against neglecting the passion and aim of catechesis because it is "too Catholic" or the highly structured form may be intimidating. A gospel-centered family views every aspect of family-life, from meal-time to matters of discipline and punishment, to help children identify the root-causes of their sin, point them to a holy Heavenly Father who has provided grace for them through Jesus Christ, and to discover their identity in Christ.[149]

Matthew Henry focuses on the big-picture impact a family can have on culture when he writes, "If there were a church in every house, there would be such a church in our land as would make it a praise throughout the whole earth. We cannot better serve our country than by keeping up religion in our families. Let families be well catechized, and then the public preaching of the word will be the more profitable, and

---

[148]Joel R Beeke, *Family Worship, 2nd Edition (family Guidance)*, 2 ed. (Grand Rapids, MI: Reformation Heritage Books, 2009); Jason Helopoulos, *Neglected Grace, A: Family Worship in the Christian Home* (Fearn, Scotland: Christian Focus, 2013).

[149]Paul David Tripp, *Parenting: the 14 Gospel Principles That Can Radically Change Your Family* (Wheaton, IL: Crossway, 2016).

the more successful."[150] In this way, the father is a type of pastor over his family and is responsible to ensure that the home is a place where Christ is loved, known, and honored. It is for this reason that Jonathan Edwards wrote, "Every Christian family ought to be as it were a little church."[151]

Viewing the family as a mini-church seems obvious and natural, and yet very few parents consistently make a deliberate effort to disciple their teenage children. Instead, it seems most rely on attempts made during their teenager's childhood and on the positive influence of others. Family discipleship while children are still young is a challenge that many Christian parents pursue, but many have given up by the teen years. In the midst of physical and developmental changes, parents and others must be steadfast in seeking the Lord to unfold His plan for each teenager so he or she might come to discover his or her identity *in Christ*. While salvation is the work of God, He chooses to work primarily through two human agents of grace: the family and the church.

The Family as a Mirror: Christ and the Church

The New Testament's most direct teaching on the family is found in Ephesians 5:21—6:9. This Scripture is replete with controversy surrounding gender roles as well as slavery since slaves are addressed as members of the household. In the midst of various interpretations, it is clear Paul is anchoring the Christian household to Christ's relationship with the Church. Wives are instructed to "*submit to your own husbands, as to the Lord. For the husband is the head of the wife even as Christ is the head of the church, his body, and is himself its Savior. Now as the church submits to Christ, so also wives should submit in everything to their husbands*" (Ephesians 5:22–24). He continues by telling husbands, "*love your wives, as*

---

[150]Henry, *Family Religion*, 53.

[151]Jonathan Edwards, "Thoughts on Revival and Religion in New England," vol. 1, *The Works of Jonathan Edwards* (Peabody, MA: Hendrickson Publishers, 1998), 419-20.

Christ loved the church and gave himself up for her, that he might sanctify her, having cleansed her by the washing of water with the word, so that he might present the church to himself in splendor, without spot or wrinkle or any such thing, that she might be holy and without blemish" (Ephesians 5:25–27).

In the Greek, the primary verb in this section is actually a present-participle in Ephesians 5:21. This word, ὑποτάσσω[152] *(hupotassō),* sets the tone for Christian households: they are built upon the calling to submit to one another out of reverence for Christ. Indeed, all of life is centered around the person and work of Jesus Christ. It is fitting for marriage and family to be a tangible expression of the love, sacrifice, and intimacy that comes through the gospel. God's forgiving, patient, selfless love is put on display through both marriage and parenting. The biblical teaching on family is consistent between the Old and New Testaments, for the family is a mirror: as the unique image-bearers of God and as a living picture of Christ's love for the Church. This is found both through common-grace in non-Christian families to the degree they reflect the biblical teachings, but it is to be an especially powerful and beautiful expression through the Christian family. This is why Paul concludes his instructions to husbands and wives by explaining, *"This mystery is profound, and I am saying that it refers to Christ and the church"* (Ephesians 5:32). Marriage is undeniably the most essential human relationship in the family, and it is anchored in creation.

Children and slaves[153] are commanded to be obedient and submissive (Ephesians 6:1, 5). Begrudging obedience and bitter submission is warned against, not because the Bible views children and slaves as less-than-human, but because the purpose of the household is to reflect

---

[152]Ephesians 5:21 includes the present participle form, 'υποτασσόμενοι, which is translated as "Submitting."

[153]Exploring the similarities and differences between slavery in the Bible and American Chattel Slavery are beyond the scope of this book, but it must be noted that they were quite different. Even in the midst of such difference, the Bible's recognition that it exists, should not be taken as approval that it continues.

Christ and the Church in all facets. Even in the sections addressing children and slaves, the father (as head and master of the family) is instructed to be kind and gentle, not harsh. Once again, the Bible's instructions for the household are given around the central affirmation that the family is intended to reflect the character of God.

In the midst of the contemporary unraveling of the family, it has become a common temptation for Christians to elevate the family beyond the teaching of Scripture. It is an over-correction of the highest degree to elevate the family above the church, as if the church exists for the sake of the family when the opposite is quite true. The church is not to be seen as a "family of families"[154] because in Christ, all Christians are one family. Singles, children, married, widows are all members of one another and come to church as one family. The local church is called to make disciples of all peoples and to baptize them as an expression of their identity as members of the family of God.

The Bible is unflinching regarding the sanctity of the family. And yet, Ephesians 5:21—6:9 makes it clear the family exists for the sake of the Church—not the other way around. The family is a visible expression of the spiritual family of God. In the scope of eternity, the "wedding supper of the Lamb" (Revelation 19:6-10), the perfect consummation of God's promises to His people, will be realized and the mirror of the family will no longer be necessary, for God's people will live with perfect intimacy in the presence of God (Matthew 22:30).

---

[154]This is a common expression among proponents of the "Family Integrated Church Movement."

The Family's Responsibility to Youth

Reputable and large-scale sociological studies have shown that children largely reflect the faith of their parents.[155] Even among nonreligious families where parents avoid religious instruction in order to permit their children to choose whatever religion seems best to them, these parents are discipling their children to believe that religion is an optional pursuit and all faiths are equally valid. Parents are the primary disciple-makers of their children, but Christian parents understand they are also members of a spiritual family, the Church. The local church serves in a similar manner as the family's clan in biblical times—as an intergenerational family who is committed to passing down faith to the next generation. Rather than viewing co-discipleship of the next generation between the family and the local church as a matter of competition or usurping parental authority, there is synergy and partnership as the church fulfills their vow to parents, made at their child's dedication (or baptism, depending on the church's doctrine).

The pressure to appear as the perfect Christian family leads many to simply build a façade of godliness while stumbling under the weight of the law. But Christ came to save sinners, not simply to give them better rules and instructions. Regardless of the offender (husband, wife, or child), when sin is evident, the family reflects Christ and the Church through open confession, repentance, and restoration. The declaration of Romans 8:1 brings great freedom, "*There is therefore now no condemnation for those who are in Christ Jesus.*" When children are raised in a household who rightly understands law and gospel there will be a wonderful sense of duty, accountability, and grace.

Allowing one's family to become so busy and overloaded that family discipleship falls by the wayside is an entirely unacceptable option for

---

[155]Bengtson, *Families and Faith*. Christian Smith and Melinda Lundquist Denton, *Soul Searching: the Religious and Spiritual Lives of American Teenagers* (Oxford, UK: Oxford University Press, 2005).

the Christian family, and yet this is where many find themselves. This requires consistency more than anything else—spending time reading a portion of Scripture, discussing it briefly, and then praying together can take as little as five minutes, but will make a great impact when it is a regular commitment. God ordained the family to serve as a mirror of His relationship with the Church. Husbands and wives love one another and their children in light of God's steadfast love for His people. When the family is centered around the gospel they will fulfill both the Creation Mandate and the Great Commission: to do all things for the honor of God and to spread His glory throughout the earth. It is therefore imperative that parents remember their biblical calling to honor God through their family.

Recent generations of parents have largely neglected their biblical responsibility to disciple their children. Among those who desire to be intentional in family discipleship, many parents grew up in a household where parents simply did not talk about religion because it was a private matter. Other parents have basically felt unequipped to answer hard questions and therefore avoid the conversation altogether. Pastors and churches are discovering that Christian parents are increasingly aware of their calling to disciple their children, but they have no framework or personal experience upon which to build, since they themselves have never been discipled.[156] Family discipleship begins with evangelism. Too many parents assume their children are converted because they grew up in church and have a good base of biblical knowledge. As parents reaffirm their commitment to family discipleship, may they remember to begin by co-evangelizing their children with the church's support.

---

[156]George Barna, *Revolutionary Parenting: What the Research Shows Really Works* (Carol Stream, IL: BarnaBooks, 2007).

Conclusion: The Family and the Family of God

By now it should be clear that today's nuclear family is not an entirely biblical concept. Accordingly, it is entirely fitting for Christian parents to rally around them other members of the family of God to co-evangelize and co-disciple their children. If the Church is the family of God and the members are given different spiritual gifts, it is a beautiful thing to see children and teenagers as recipients of those gifts being exercised. A church's youth ministry should not be viewed as usurping parental authority, but as a ministry to teenagers by men and women who are spiritual family-members.

A biblical theology of the family paints a beautiful picture of the family as a living embodiment of Christ and the Church. Godly families are centered around the love and grace that God has given to His children through Jesus Christ. It is unfortunate and unbiblical to set the disciple-making mission of the family aside in exchange for building a large youth ministry. It is also unbiblical to prioritize family-discipleship to the point that the family of faith has nothing to contribute to children and adolescents' spiritual development. Both the Church and the family were created by God to multiply faithful worshippers—may this become an increasingly shared mission.

Chapter 7

The Gospel and Youth Ministry

Without the gospel there is no Church, no Christian, and no salvation. The gospel is the announcement of good news and rescue for sinners who could not save themselves by law-keeping. John 3:16-17 famously declares, *"For God so loved the world, that he gave his only Son, that whoever believes in him should not perish but have eternal life. For God did not send his Son into the world to condemn the world, but in order that the world might be saved through him."* This must be the central message of youth ministry because it is the central message of Scripture. Without saving faith in the gospel, students might have healthy relationships with their family and peers, good grades, and make generally wise choices but still be completely and utterly lost. Every other benefit the church has to offer can be found elsewhere—friends, service projects, morality, etc. Salvation is by faith alone in Christ alone through the grace of God alone. Wise and discerning youth workers guard carefully against false expectations that lead to mission drift; away from being centered on the gospel.

Every Christian would freely admit the gospel is essential for fruitful ministry to teenagers. Confusion abounds, however, regarding what it means to minister to teenagers in light of the gospel. Some claim that generations of youth workers have essentially neglected the gospel and that youth ministry needs a radical overhaul, while others agree there has been too much emphasis on entertainment but disagree the gospel has been absent and are working to reform the youth ministry world from within. In many ways, these two approaches reflect the different efforts to reform the English Church by the Puritans and the Pilgrims. Whereas the Puritans sought reformation from within the English Church, the Pilgrims launched a new church movement where they could implement the reforms they believed were necessary. Both parties agreed with the need for reformation of the English Church, and both approaches to reforming youth ministry today agree the gospel has largely been overshadowed by either entertainment or self-help-Christianity. Regardless of one's approach to reform, the argument of this book is to examine Scripture and ask the question, "What does the Bible and historic Christian teaching have to say about ministry to teenagers?" Regardless of one's allegiances within the broader youth ministry world, it should be agreed upon by all that biblically faithful youth ministry must be gospel-centered. Before moving toward clarity on what gospel-centered youth ministry looks like, it is first necessary to get clarity on the gospel itself.

The Gospel

Much of the confusion regarding what it means to be gospel-centered has come from a fuzziness surrounding the gospel itself. Many assume that being a gospel-centered youth worker means every message is the same Easter story every week. Instead, gospel-centered youth workers operate out of a biblical theology that understands Jesus as the fulfillment of salvation history (Luke 24:27; Galatians 3:8), and then calls students to repent of their sin because of the gracious love of God that is theirs by faith in Jesus Christ.

The Narrow and Broad Gospel

Students are not transformed by their parents' or youth pastor's wisdom, but by the power of God. When the family and the church are committed to gospel-centered ministry, everything is soaked in the grace of God. God's law is not absent, or even set aside, but it is taught in order to show teenagers their need for a Savior. Law and gospel must always be taught together. Instead of this approach, most children and youth ministry resources can be summarized as, "Be a good person." This simply is not Christian teaching and dishonors the Word of God. Instead of teaching Christian moralism, biblical youth ministry emphasizes the narrow and the broad gospel. The narrow gospel is the proclamation of Jesus Christ's death and resurrection in order to redeem and secure the people of God by grace through faith. This is announcement of salvation and is highlighted in the evangelistic invitation to be saved from sin and judgment into new life as a child of God. The broader gospel grounds the believer in a worldview saturated by the grace of God and points to the unfolding of salvation history: Creation, Fall, Redemption, and Glorification. The middle chapters of salvation history (Fall and Redemption) receive the most attention in today's church because they emphasize the current realities of sin and brokenness and the transforming power of the gospel to save and redeem. While the narrow gospel highlights the person and work of Jesus Christ through the cross and empty tomb, the broad gospel anchors the Christian in the reality that all Scripture and all of life find their fulfillment in Jesus Christ. Whereas the narrow gospel is individualistic due to the personal need for faith and repentance, the broad gospel tends to emphasize the communal identity of the Christian within the totality of God's grand work of salvation. Focusing too heavily on the broad gospel while underemphasizing the narrow will lead to good biblical theology at the expense of personal faith and relationship with Jesus Christ. Today's tendency to focus almost entirely on the narrow gospel has led to a generation of Christians whose failure to understand the broader gospel has led to individualistic faith that is theologically under-developed. It is interesting to observe that the Early Church largely began their evangelism and catechesis with the broader gospel (see chapter 4), while churches today view that as something for mature believers.

The New Testament word that is consistently translated "gospel" is the Greek word, εὐαγγέλιον (*euangelion*), which means "good news, glad tidings." When the New Testament mentions the preaching of the gospel, the verb εὐαγγελίζω (*euangelizō*) is used rather the more generic κηρύσσω (*kērussō*), meaning "preach." Instead, εὐαγγελίζω emphasizes the particular act of declaring the gospel so sinners would repent and receive the grace of God through Jesus Christ. The emphasis of the Greek εὐαγγελίζω (*euangelizō*) is still carried through to today's English word "evangelism." Jesus understood His own mission to be one of accomplishing and announcing the good news of the Kingdom of God (Luke 4:18). Gospel proclamation is the central ministry of the Apostles throughout the New Testament (Acts 5:42, 14:15; Romans 15:20; Galatians 1:16). Whereas the "good news" was a generic phrase used in Rabbinic Judaism regarding God's blessing on His people, Paul's frequent "use of *tó euangélion* shows that the concept is now a fixed one both for himself and his readers."[157] The message of the gospel is rooted in history (Christ's life, death, resurrection, and ascension), but Scripture applies the fruit of those events to those who were not actually present. Thus, the gospel has been entrusted to the Church as a proclamation of good news for all peoples (Matthew 28:18-20; Acts 1:8).

Youth workers must continue to preach the gospel for both evangelism and teaching, reflecting both the narrow and the broader gospel so teenagers would grow a faith that is both personal (narrow) and deep enough to shape a Christian worldview (broad). Ray Ortlund ex-

---

[157]G. Friedrich, "εὐαγγέλιον" *Theological Dictionary of the New Testament: Abridged in One Volume* (Grand Rapids, MI: Wm. B. Eerdmans, 1985), 270.

plains the essential message of the gospel this way, "God, through the perfect life, atoning death, and bodily resurrection of Jesus Christ, rescues all his people from the wrath of God into peace with God, with a promise of the full restoration of his created order forever—all to the praise of the glory of his grace."[158] Ortlund captures the gospel in both its narrow and broad senses in a way that helpfully demonstrates the faithful gospel declaration needed in pastoral ministry. By emphasizing that youth ministries should consistently proclaim the gospel, this exhortation is pointed at a regular proclamation both the narrow and the broad gospel, not only the narrow.[159]

The Only Message of Salvation

Given the cultural climate of GenZ, it is important for youth workers to teach the exclusivity of the gospel with clarity and humility. After a survey of students who graduated from my youth ministry over a twelve-year period I discovered while many students agreed with the statement, "Salvation is found only through Jesus Christ," those who graduated in the last five years were increasingly adhering to what is known as *Christian Universalism.*[160] This is a belief that, as I worded it in the survey, "Jesus is the only savior and He will save everyone, whether they believe in him or not." By agreeing with this statement, those who grew up in the church were able to consider themselves Christians and affirm many doctrinal truths in a way that sounds historically orthodox, all while embracing modern views on tolerance and pluralism. Due to the cultural atmosphere of youth culture, it is very easy for a gos-

---

[158]Ray Ortlund, *The Gospel: How the Church Portrays the Beauty of Christ* (Wheaton, IL: Crossway, 2014), 16.

[159]The best example of cultural engagement of "felt needs" that points the reader to the narrow and broad gospel is Tim Keller's book *Counterfeit Gods.* See: Timothy Keller, *Counterfeit Gods: The Empty Promises of Money, Sex, and Power and the Only Hope that Matters* (New York, NY: Penguin Books, 2009).

[160]This was not a scientific study, but it accords with sociological research about the priority of tolerance among GenZ.

pel-preaching, grace-heavy ministry to unintentionally produce Christian Universalists. Youth workers should not shy away from preaching the gospel of grace, but they must also be careful to teach the whole counsel of God.

Christian Universalism does not find support through the teachings of Jesus, who taught that God will judge and some *"will go away into eternal punishment, but the righteous into eternal life"* (Matthew 25:46). In the Sermon on the Mount, He taught about the reality of damnation, saying, *"Enter by the narrow gate. For the gate is wide and the way is easy that leads to destruction, and those who enter by it are many"* (Matthew 7:13). Jesus taught frequently on hell (Matthew 10:28, 5:29-30, 23:15, 33; Luke 10:15, 16:23), which would be quite strange if His mission was to save every person. Rather than denying the coming judgment, Jesus preached the gospel: *"Truly, truly, I say to you, whoever hears my word and believes him who sent me has eternal life. He does not come into judgment, but has passed from death to life"* (John 5:24). It is notable that Jesus said *"whoever hears my words and believes him who sent me."* Jesus also said, *"If anyone does not abide in me he is thrown away like a branch and withers; and the branches are gathered, thrown into the fire, and burned"* (John 15:6). Affirmation of Christian Universalism demands disagreement with Jesus Christ Himself.

Perhaps the clearest statement in the Gospels comes in John 14:6 where Jesus declares, *"I am the way, and the truth, and the life. No one comes to the Father except through me"* (John 14:6). Peter's preaching in Acts 4:12 points to the exclusivity of Christ for salvation but could leave the door open for Christian Universalists. Paul closes that door and locks it shut by writing,

> *"For 'everyone who calls on the name of the Lord will be saved.' How then will they call on him in whom they have not believed? And how are they to believe in him of whom they have never heard? And how are*

*they to hear without someone preaching? And how are they to preach
unless they are sent? As it is written, "How beautiful are the feet of
those who preach the good news!"*
(Romans 10:13–15)

The obvious challenge facing parents and youth workers is differentiating genuine adherence to the gospel with this Christian Universalism, and being equipped to respond biblically and with gentleness. This is not a new challenge or temptation. Larry Hurtado describes the following regarding the earliest generations of Christians, "Among the particular features that distinguished Christianity from traditional 'pagan' religious practice and from the many other new religious movements of the time was the firm insistence that there is only one 'true and living God,' and the demand that its adherents had to drop all worship of any other deity."[161] Christians in the Early Church serve as a faithful example of holding out the invitation of the gospel in the face of violent pressure to conform to religious pluralism. The exclusivity of the gospel both challenges today's culture while fueling the faithful youth worker to proclaim the gospel to every student.

Repentance and the Gospel

Many evangelists seem to operate under the impression that theological maturity is necessary for discipleship but is optional for evangelism. This is most evidently displayed through doctrinally thin "gospel invitations" that are light on doctrinal truth, and at times even devoid of it. It is common to hear gospel presentations at youth conferences where the cross and resurrection are hardly mentioned at all and where a call to repentance is entirely absent. Youth workers rarely talk about "proclaiming the gospel" and more frequently talk about how they "share the gospel" or give a "gospel invitation." Evangelists unasham-

---

[161]Larry W. Hurtado, *Destroyer of the Gods: Early Christian Distinctiveness in the Roman World* (Waco, TX: Baylor University Press, 2016), 37-38.

edly declare the gospel and call sinners to repentance, or else they are not evangelists at all.

Among the gravest concerns that has become evident in student evangelism is the absence of repentance. The most common response called for is confession or a vague invitation to "receive Jesus." Repentance is rarely mentioned as a response to the gospel. Instead, evangelists seem to indicate that wanting the fruit of the gospel (salvation, forgiveness of sin, eternal hope, etc.) is tantamount to becoming a Christian. Desiring salvation is not the same thing as receiving it. First John 1:5-10 makes two things clear: First, the Bible holds out confession and repentance as the biblical response to the gospel; and second, Christians must walk in the light of righteousness, or they are liars and are not children of God at all. This is not works-righteousness, but living fruit of the grace of God at work in the Christian. Perhaps the reason so many students who raise their hand at camps and conferences walk away from the faith is because they were never converted in the first place. Grace was promised too quickly. They responded to the gospel by expressing, "Yes, I want that!" but they never understood the call to confession and repentance. Rather than pressing students for an immediate response, the type of catechesis "Inquirers" received in the Early Church might be worth reconsidering – namely, clear instruction on both the narrow and the broad gospel.

There are two types of confession, both of which are important forerunners of biblical repentance. To confess simply means to admit or agree that something is true. With this in mind, there are two truths that must be confessed before someone can become a Christian: first, sin and the rightful judgment that comes from it must be confessed (see 1 John 1:9), and second, Jesus Christ is the Son of God and Savior (see Romans 10:9). These confessions prompt biblical repentance.

Martin Luther famously wrote in the first of his 95 Theses, "When our Lord and Master Jesus Christ said 'Repent,' He willed the entire life of believers to be one of repentance."[162] The Christian life is composed of daily repentance because sin has already been atoned for and grace has been applied; there is no further need for either shame or works-righteousness. The Greek μετάνοια (*metánoia*) literally means "to change one's mind" that leads to change in behavior. Repentance, at its core, evokes the imagery of a soldier doing an about-face. Rather than continuing in one line of thought or action, repentance issues a recognition that a change is necessary and does it. Conversion, then, involves confession ("I am a great sinner"), profession of faith ("God is a great savior through Jesus Christ"), and is followed by repentance ("My life is not my own, but now belongs to God and I will live for him"). Confession, profession, and repentance do not necessarily take place in the chronological order, as if there is significant time in between. Rather, they are a logical way to think through the layers of what it means to become a Christian.

Within the gospel-centered movement, repentance seems like a controversial doctrine because it seems law-driven rather than gospel-driven. In a way, it is easier to teach repentance from a law-driven approach that shows students their sin, teaches them the commandments of God, and then calls for repentance by essentially saying "try harder." The problem with this approach is that repentance requires the power of God, not the will of man. The gospel fuels repentance by inviting sinners to stop their striving to fix themselves and calling them to live in the freedom of Christ's grace. As Galatians 5:13 explains, "For you were called to freedom, brothers. Only do not use your freedom as an opportunity for the flesh, but through love serve one another." The grace of God is what makes repentance possible. There is no guilt or shame in repentance, because the Christian knows God's grace has already atoned for sin and his or her status before God is entirely secure.

---

[162]Martin Luther, "95 Theses," in Timothy F. Lull, *Martin Luther's Basic Theological Writings*, (Minneapolis, MN: Fortress Press, 1989), 21.

The gospel proclaims grace and hope to those who are burdened under the crushing weight of trying to prove themselves, to earn love and respect, and to make their life mean something (Matthew 11:29). It reduces insecurity to dust in the light of Jesus' promise that no one can snatch His sheep from His hand (John 10:27-28) and seals him or her as a member of the family of God by the indwelling Holy Spirit (Ephesians 1:13-14). Repentance does not add works to the gospel of grace, but demonstrates that joyful obedience is the fruit of the new life that comes by faith in Jesus Christ. The preaching of the gospel calls students to confession and repentance as they hear the good news of the life, death, resurrection, ascension, and eventual return of Christ to rescue sinners.

Because the gospel is the only message of salvation, biblical ministry to students must be firmly built on a gospel foundation. Without the gospel, any partnership between the family and the church will only result in a well-behaved generation who remains separated from God.

Gospel-Centered Youth Ministry

Cameron Cole captures the need for youth workers to revisit the role of the gospel in their ministry to students by writing, "Traditionally, youth ministry methodology demonstrated a specific theology about kids' biggest problem. It suggested that kids lack both proper knowledge about moral Christian living and sufficient motivation to adhere to the standards. The kids would do right if they just knew how to obey God, and if they had consistent reinforcement to 'be good Christians.'"[163] Out of a desire to help students live as faithful disciples, youth workers are easily tempted to lead with the law rather than the gospel, but the law has never saved anyone. In youth ministry's effort

---

163   Cameron Cole, "The Gospel at the Heart of All Things: Youth Ministry Founded in the Gospel," Cameron Cole and Jon Nielson, eds., *Gospel-Centered Youth Ministry: A Practical Guide* (Wheaton, IL: Crossway, 2016), 26.

to shape a generation, students have been given practical advice about the Bible's teaching on various topics, while the gospel has been viewed as an evangelistic tool.

Students need more than biblical counsel about sexuality, friendship, family, and technology. One can hardly imagine fruitful pastoral ministry to teenagers that does not touch upon those topics, but teenagers' greatest need is the same as everyone else's: they need to be reconciled to God. Parents can put pressure on youth workers to help address behavior problems, and youth workers can be so eager to help students with their daily issues that sin is only discussed in specific ways. For instance, when a student is struggling with pornography it is much easier to discuss accountability relationships and internet filters to help minimize future offenses than it is to address the cravings that fuel the temptation in the first place. In this example, the specific sin of lust is addressed, but innate sinful cravings and the disbelief in the satisfying joy of union with Christ remain silent. Better filters and increased self-control are not the balm for those who battle sexual temptations. The gospel sets a spotlight on human sin and declares, "God saves sinners. Will you confess your sin, profess faith in Jesus Christ's victory over sin and death, walk the path of repentance, and drink deeply from the cup of grace?" When teenagers behold the beauty of God and discover the intimacy of God's love for sinners, sexual temptations will probably not disappear, but they'll be recognized for what they are: accusation that God cannot bring more happiness than sex. If youth workers only understand the gospel as an evangelistic message they will address students' sexual sins with a combination of psychological and technological resources, but a gospel-centered youth worker will primarily respond by pointing teens to the nature and beauty of God and then possibly employ other resources as secondary measures.

This past decade of ministry in the evangelical Christian church has brought about a growing concern about being "gospel-centered."

In many important ways, this is a welcome shift. At the same time, this phrase has become so nebulous and ambiguous it has become common to see ministries and resourced self-described as *gospel-centered* that are anything but. As unpopular and potentially arrogant as it may seem, it is important to recognize that not all *gospel-centered* ministries are created equal. In an effort to gain clarity on the central role of the gospel in youth ministry, it may first be helpful to address three postures youth ministries may take regarding the gospel: gospel-absent, gospel-present, and gospel-centered.

Three Approaches to Youth Ministry and the Gospel

Ministries can fall into a gospel-absent approach in one of two ways—intentionally or accidentally. The first camp views Jesus as purely a motivational figure who inspires men and women to live better lives. This is the Jesus of the social gospel, health and wealth churches, and other similar movements within liberal Christianity. In this sense, the gospel is more about building heaven on earth and living your best life now than it is a proclamation of the restoration of *shalom* through the life, death, and resurrection of Jesus Christ. The gospel certainly involves pursuing justice for the oppressed, but Jesus' words to His disciples in Matthew 26:11[164] are worth remembering. Ministries who fall into the category do so by misunderstanding the gospel in such a way they fundamentally reject historic Christianity by pursuing the Kingdom on Earth rather than the Kingdom of Heaven.

The second camp within gospel-absent ministry, is more subtle. The drift progresses undercover while youth leaders are trying to be relevant, helpful, and approachable to teenagers. Of course, those are important values in youth workers and do not always lead toward gospel-absentness, but they provide the setting for the drift to take place.

---

[164]"For you always have the poor with you, but you will not always have me." (Matthew 26:11, ESV)

Since teenagers are coming of age in a post-Christian world, the common assumption is that emphasizing too much "Jesus talk" and Bible-teaching will bore students, seem irrelevant, and turn young people away. Therefore, those critical emphases are lost or marginalized. In an effort to make Christianity accessible, the Bible is often viewed as an owner's manual and is taught in a way that helps teenagers understand how God wants His people to live. This approach twists the Bible into a rule book and presents the gospel as a new law. But the gospel is a proclamation of good news, for it announces salvation for sinners through faith in the life, death, resurrection, and return of Jesus Christ. Despite the wonderful intentions, the gospel is absent because these ministries, in their desire to be relevant and helpful, have become law centered. The gospel is reduced to a general exhortation of loving others, morality, and being "good Christians." This is a warped gospel and not what was proclaimed by Jesus or the apostles. As tempting as it may be to either vilify those in this camp or to overlook their law-centered approach because it came from good motives, those who have drifted into gospel-absent ministry are hereby invited to recognize the drift that has taken place and rebuild on the gospel.

The second way ministries can relate to the gospel is probably the most common approach among evangelical Christians: gospel-present ministry. There is a common assumption that ministries who preach the gospel, hold to historic and orthodox doctrine, and do evangelism are therefore gospel-centered. Many godly youth workers fall into this category. They preach the gospel of salvation by grace alone, through faith alone. But the gospel is largely disconnected from their discipleship strategy and is viewed as a doorway that is essential for entrance into salvation in this life and into glory in the next. The gospel has increasingly become an evangelistic tool that is treated as the entryway into the family of God (initial salvation) and as the exit (final salvation into glory), but the gospel has not shaped youth workers' daily understanding of what it means to be a Christian: an adopted and beloved child of God (regardless of his/her unworthiness). Gospel-present youth workers would benefit to recall Paul's words in Galatians 3:3, "*Are you so foolish? Having begun by the Spirit, are you now being perfected by the flesh?*" The gospel is not a doorway into and out of the Christian life, but the lifeblood itself.

Confidence in the Holy Spirit to bear the fruit of ministry may not be absent, but youth workers too easily trust in their ability and ministry plans more than they want to admit. In the broader youth ministry world, discipleship is more about providing godly counsel and life advice than it is about helping students understand God's Word. When the gospel is present but not central, youth workers may be preaching the narrow gospel for salvation while overlooking the broader gospel's impact for discipleship and worldview development.

Ministry effectiveness is not dependent on whether or not youth group went well last week, but upon the power of God at work in students' lives. While many agree with that statement theologically, their ministry practices deny it. Gospel-present ministries often cater more to the assumed preferences of teenagers than on simple, consistent, and confident teaching of Scripture. Teaching has fallen out of favor in many youth groups, because students supposedly don't like being talked at and have a short attention span. This is popularly conveyed through the saying that teenagers need a "guide on the side" rather than a "sage on the stage." But this sets up a false dichotomy and completely overlooks the biblical emphasis (and example) on preaching and teaching. The Apostle Paul wrote, "*For Christ did not send me to baptize but to preach the gospel, and not with words of eloquent wisdom, lest the cross of Christ be emptied of its power. For the word of the cross is folly to those who are perishing, but to us who are being saved it is the power of God*" (1 Corinthians 1:17-18). Paul's example demonstrates a value for being culturally aware (Acts 17:16-34) even while challenging cultural values through trust in the power of God to do the persuading rather than trusting in being his own cultural savvy or relevance. Stories and illustrations are good teaching tools, so long as they highlight the main point rather than overtake it. Far too often, gospel-present youth workers assume students will be bored by God's Word, so they distill a biblical truth while incorporating a few Scripture references or two while incorporating some attention-grabbing story or illustration that overshadows the biblical message. Of course, few gospel-present youth workers would agree they rely more on their presentation or on their cool-factor than they rely on the authority of the Word of God. But if the Bible is the inspired and authoritative Word of God, then youth workers should teach it with confidence that God will continue to build his Church (which includes teenagers) through it.

Because there is no hope for salvation without the gospel, it is incumbent upon church leaders and parents to partner through a gospel-centered youth ministry. The defining mark between gospel-present and gospel-centered youth ministry is whether or not the gospel is central in every facet of the ministry or merely on the periphery. The gospel must shape more than the evangelism of a ministry. Instead, it is the DNA that shapes every facet of ministry—from games to calendar planning to Bible Study. The following section unpacks the five pillars of a gospel-centered youth ministry, as expressed by the Rooted Ministry.[165]

Five Pillars of Gospel-Centered Youth Ministry

Pillar 1: Gospel Centrality

Gospel centrality is a welcome emphasis in the world of youth ministry. Youth ministry has consistently demonstrated a commitment to

---

[165] *The Rooted Ministry* has defined five pillars that are natural and essential pillars for gospel-centered youth ministry. With their permission, the following is an exploration of these pillars. Visit Rooted at rootedministry.com.

evangelism, and yet discipleship of teenagers is in need of the same rebuke Paul issued in Galatians 3:3, "*Are you so foolish? Having begun by the Spirit, are you now being perfected by the flesh?*" The narrow gospel has often been held out through evangelism while the broader gospel has often been absent from the way youth workers disciple students. Students are increasingly suffering from crippling anxiety and depression and both the narrow and broad gospel deliver the grace and peace and hope that is so desperately needed. The gospel proclaims grace to the sinners, peace to the anxious, and hope for the depressed. Gospel-centered youth ministry invites students to discover intimacy with God for which humanity was created through faith in the gospel, because through it they are receive the same love the Father lavished upon the Son (John 17:20-23). Why would anyone push this message to the sidelines in exchange for fun and games or dating advice? Instead, all other topics and activities are viewed through the lens of the narrow and broad gospel. Gospel-centered youth workers are diligent to ensure that every message they deliver highlights the gospel, in either the narrow or broad sense. They regularly ask themselves, "Did Jesus need to die and rise from the grave for me to teach this lesson or give this counsel?" In this way, the entire youth ministry is built around the gospel (narrow and broad), and anything that is not clearly built upon the gospel is either reformed or eliminated.

When youth workers remember the grace they have received they will seek to build a culture of grace throughout their youth ministry. In this way, the gospel produces a culture of grace that extends beyond the formal teaching times and shapes the atmosphere of the group. This culture of grace extends even to the game nights and fun activities that help strengthen relationships within the group rather than breeding competition and rivalry. Students are free to come as they are rather than pretending to be put together. Sin is not overlooked and is dealt with seriously, because grace has removed guilt and shame. The walls that so easily divide students according to ethnicity, family backgrounds, income, and what school they attend will crumble because students are consistently reminded they are united through a shared faith in Jesus Christ. Servanthood and ministry become hallmarks of the group's identity, not because students need to fulfill community-service hours, but because the gospel frees the Christian to do good works for their neighbor as an expression of God's sacrificial love.

The grace of God is the engine of a gospel-centered youth ministry. Rather than producing a highly impressive show to get students to come, youth workers simply proclaim the gospel and embody the love and grace of God to the best of their ability. The gospel is on the main-stage at all times. Rather than driving students to fix their behavior, youth workers invite them to become children of God through what Christ has done on their behalf, knowing that the Holy Spirit will reshape their hearts and desires as they understand their identity in Christ. Every other pillar may be present in a ministry, but without clarity on gospel centrality, those students will be receiving some form of behavior modification rather than the gospel of grace.

Pillar 2: Theological Depth Through Expository, Biblical Teaching

Because the Bible is "breathed out by God and profitable for teaching, for reproof, for correction, and for training in righteousness, that the man of God may be complete, equipped for every good work" (2 Timothy 3:16–17), youth workers must not be ashamed to keep it front-and-center. It is strange how many youth workers hold to an orthodox view of Scripture while rejecting expository teaching as out of touch and irrelevant for teenagers. This is one of the main areas where a youth worker's *stated theology* and their *actual theology* unintentionally differ. Either the Bible is the inspired, authoritative Word of God, or it is not. And if it is, then it should be the primary emphasis in a youth ministry's teaching. This does not excuse sloppy teaching or droning lectures. It is good teaching to embrace various learning strategies and respect students' short attention spans. But gospel-centered youth workers teach the Word of God as sufficient and authoritative, even for teenagers.

Relevance is not something to be laid on top of the sermon, but something to be called out from within the text itself. Dietrich Bonhoeffer's instructions for seminary students preparing for ministry in Nazi Germany are helpful for youth workers to consider. Because the world constantly shifts and changes, Bonhoeffer encourages using a nonreligious language that recognizes the universality of the human condition while also adjusting to the social and cultural changes. He wrote, "The Church must come out of its stagnation. We must move out again into the open air of intellectual discussion with the world, and risk saying controversial things, if we are to get down to the serious problems of life."[166] These "controversial things" are not to be understood as "un-Christian" or only "slightly biblical" things. Rather, Bonhoeffer instructed his students to speak God's words even when they were completely counter-cultural to the contemporary narrative. It is a call to embrace the complexity of Christian faithfulness in a world that considers God irrelevant and unnecessary. In many ways, youth workers are the tip of the spear in the Church's engagement with the broader culture. Youth workers are often the first leaders in the church who must address controversial issues, such as sexual identity and transgenderism. In seeking to be relevant, preachers and youth workers alike are often tempted to deliver an abstract and theoretical, rather than a genuinely concrete, word. Because Scripture is true, it is already relevant with or without added fanfare. Again, Bonhoeffer exhorts, "The most essential element of the Christian message and of textual exposition is not a human act of interpretation but is always none other than

---

[166]Dietrich Bonhoeffer, *Letters and Papers From Prison.* ed. Eberhard Bethge, trans. Reginald Fuller, Frandk Clark and others (New York, NY: Touchstone, 1971), 200.

God, it is the Holy Spirit."[167] Faithful youth workers rely on the Holy Spirit, not on their cultural savvy or pedagogical prowess, to the build the Church and draw students to saving faith in Jesus Christ. The youth worker's task, then, is to so understand the world of teenagers and the biblical text that the Word of God is brought to bear on the particular teenagers in his or her ministry, and then to deliver it with pastoral care and conviction.

An emphasis on biblical, expository teaching in youth ministry reflects the biblical and historical example outlined in previous chapters. God's people are called to teach and instruct the young so they would know and understand God's mighty works. Leading a youth ministry that is faithful to biblical teaching reflects what is seen in the Old and New Testaments: the teaching of God's Word to the young and modeling for them what it looks like in daily life. Gospel-centered youth ministry is unashamedly built upon the authority of the Bible and teaches sound doctrine to teenagers in order that they might develop a mature, lifelong faith.

Pillar 3: Relational Discipleship

Instead of viewing themselves as "adult friends," youth workers benefit from seeing themselves as catechists of the church who focus their ministry toward those who are transitioning from childhood into adulthood. As Chapter 4 demonstrated, catechesis was a structured and highly relational ministry. Too many youth workers assume they need to choose between structured ministry or relational warmth. Because most youth workers are volunteers, it is common for them to place a high emphasis on cultivating relationships with students while overlooking the value a time-tested structure like catechesis because they

---

[167]Dietrich Bonhoeffer, "The Interpretation of the New Testament," *A Testament to Freedom*, Geffrey B. Kelly and F. Burton Nelson, eds. Revised Edition (San Francisco, CA: HarperSanFrancisco, 1995), 152.

have never been equipped for that type of ministry. As Chapter 5 emphasized, teenagers do not simply belong to the nuclear family but to the broader community as the family of God. Gospel-centered youth workers do not rely on programming for their discipleship efforts, though programs like youth groups or Bible studies are obviously good and helpful. Instead, they take a genuine interest in students' lives outside of youth group and pursue opportunities for more personal conversations that express the love of God and lead to spiritual formation.

Unfortunately, many youth workers get trapped in a cycle of friendship and never begin asking more personal questions. If youth workers never ask uncomfortable and personal questions and conversations remain on the surface level, then discipleship is not happening. Again, if the Scripture is never a significant part of the conversation between students and youth workers, then there may be a strong relationship of trust but they do not have a discipling relationship. Well-equipped youth workers have a discipleship plan and take initiative to invite students to clarify what to expect when they meet together. They may choose to read through a book of the Bible, use a catechism, memorize Scripture together, or read a good Christian book together, or any number of other plans—but without a plan, discipleship will likely never happen.

Relationship-building is where youth ministry has been strongest for decades. Sometimes, however, youth workers can become emotionally dependent on students in ways that are unhealthy and potentially even dangerous. When this happens the students become the ones who lead the relationship and set the expectations. Youth workers are called to be mentors who come alongside parents on behalf of the church leadership to co-evangelize and co-disciple the next generation. A commitment to relational discipleship requires the desire for a real relationships, not simply an impersonal meeting where an adult instructs a teenager. But in an effort to correct the perceived authoritative and impersonal ministries of former generations, youth workers can easily find themselves adopting the posture of a peer rather than embracing their role as a mentor. Youth workers must not try to win students into relationship with themselves, but with Christ. Keeping this in mind at all times will guide and guard youth workers in relational ministry. Faithful youth workers share in Paul's refrain, "*Be imitators of me, as I am of Christ*" (1 Corinthians 11:1).

Finally, in addition to the one-on-one relational component to youth ministry, the large group gatherings are also marked by a commitment to biblical fellowship. Rather than building regular youth ministry programming around high energy events, gospel-centered youth workers seek to lead groups to foster a culture soaked in the gospel of grace. There are some games that may be great fun, but do little to foster a culture of biblical fellowship and unity. Fun is not the enemy, but neither is it the savior ("if we had more fun, students would come") or purpose (like the parent who only asks, "Did you have fun at youth group?"). Because relationships matter, the youth ministry programming is planned in a way that promotes meaningful relationships between students who would otherwise never become friends. The gospel prompts youth workers to make disciples while building a culture where students grow in their love for one another (even if they attend rival schools).

Pillar 4: Partnership With Parents

Youth ministry has always recognized the important role of parents, but in all honestly, parents have often been viewed with suspicion. In a recent survey of youth pastors, 23% reported that increasing parental involvement in their teenager's spiritual development is a priority even while 34% identified a lack of parental interest as a challenge, and yet only 28% are optimistic about increasing the number of parents involved over the next three years.[168] This hardly paints a hopeful future for the partnership between the church and families for collaboration through the youth ministry. Among the chief reasons behind such disheartening statistics is the reality that many youth workers only hear from parents when there is a problem, and many parents only hear from youth workers when they need something or a payment deadline is approaching. Correcting this breakdown is foundational to biblical youth ministry. This emphasis is further elaborated in Chapter 8, which is focused on helping youth workers become bridge-builders who unite the church and family in co-evangelism and co-discipleship of the next generation.

Conflict with parents often comes from a concerned parent who is trying to advocate for their son or daughter. This should be affirmed and welcomed, even if their expression of concern is shared in the wrong way. Because gospel-centered youth workers are committed to partnering with the family, a gentle spirit will go far in cultivating trust and open communication with parents—especially when a situation could otherwise turn volatile.

Some youth workers are so committed to students, they view time with parents as time taken away from students. Nothing could be further from the truth. Remember that when students graduate from the youth ministry, they will not graduate from their family; so intentionality about collaborating with parents is a long-term investment in students. When the generations of the church are together (church picnics, potlucks, or simply in the foyer between services on Sunday morning), youth workers would be wise to spend some time with parents, not only with students. This demonstrates care for them and builds mutual trust and respect. As trust is cultivated and conversations deepen, opportu-

---

[168]The Barna Group, *The State of Youth Ministry*, 11.

nities to invest in parents and to give them a gospel-fueled vision for their teenager will only increase.

Pillar 5: Intergenerational Integration

It should be clear by now, considering the biblical foundations poured through Chapters 2 and 3, that children and youth should join their parents in the worship service and be given the opportunity to participate. Creating age-specific worship venues that separate generations during gathered worship, aside from childcare and ministry to young children, simply have no biblical foundation. Even more, they seem to be the exact opposite of what the Bible presents as normative for worship. This does not preclude discipleship or evangelism ministries from being more age-specific, but the worship of God's people should be an expression of their shared faith in Christ Jesus.

One of the great ironies of the modern church is the amount of effort expended to reach teenagers with the gospel only for them to be trained to stay away from the gathered worship of God's people. This is exactly what often takes place when they are kept apart from intergenerational worship and sent into their own age-specific program. Why would anyone expect them to view the church as a place where they belong when they have always been separated? Mark Cannister describes it this way,

> The pattern then becomes one in which children grow up in a "children's church," then move into the "middle school church," and then to the "high school church." The tragic result of this trend is that students graduate from high school having outgrown the "high school church" and having rarely experienced an intergenerational worship service or "adult church" and they have no place to go. If they go to college, they may replace their student ministry with college Christian fellowship but rarely attend church. Once they graduate from college, with

few age-appropriate options remaining, these emerging adults find themselves orphan Christians without a faith community.[169]

It should not surprise anyone when teenagers disappear from church if they have primarily grown their faith in the youth group. In some cases, it would be a stretch to say they ever attended church at all—many have attended youth group instead of church on Sunday mornings. Not only does this approach effectively train the next generation to avoid the church's gathered worship service, it is simply unbiblical and undermines nearly every biblical teaching explored in the earlier chapters. The only exception when this is an appropriate practice is when there a language barrier that necessarily separates the generations, most commonly in Asian and Latino churches throughout America.

Through faith in the gospel, all Christians are united through Christ. Because there are no junior members of the Church, gospel-centered youth workers are intentional to ensure teenagers are not merely welcomed at church, but seen as valued contributors. Creating opportunities for students and adults in the church to build friendships and get to know each other should be seen as a vital aspect of the church's ministry to teenagers. The Fuller Youth Institute has been a great champion of this vision through their *Sticky Faith* initiatives and, most recently, through *Growing Young*.[170] These books have consistently argued for a biblical foundation for age-specific ministry, but not nearly as often as is seen in today's church culture. What has become dangerously commonplace is a consumer-oriented expectation that ev-

---

[169]Mark Cannister, *Teenagers Matter: Making Student Ministry a Priority in the Church*, Youth, Family, and Culture (Grand Rapids, MI: Baker Academic, 2013), 116.

[170]Kara Eckmann Powell, Brad M. Griffin, and Cheryl A. Crawford, *Sticky Faith: Practical Ideas to Nurture Long-Term Faith in Teenagers*, youth worker ed. (Grand Rapids, MI: Zondervan, 2011). Kara Powell, *Growing Young: Six Essential Strategies to Help Young People Discover and Love Your Church* (Grand Rapids, MI: Baker, 2016).

ery generation will have their own ministry infrastructure where their particular needs will be met. Instead of catering to this consumerism, church leaders would be wise to consider how to effectively pastor the various generations while embracing a default toward bringing the generations together.

Conclusion: The Gospel and Youth Ministry

The gospel is the lifeblood of the Church. Without it, the Church dies and people remain under the judgment of God. It is a message too important to be relegated to the periphery. When youth workers build every facet of their ministry around the gospel, there will be less obsession on attendance and more emphasis on helping students grow in the grace of God through Jesus Christ. Pastoral ministry to teenagers and adults have much in common—both need the gospel, both need to be intentionally discipled, and both require great patience and wisdom in pastoral care. Rather than falling into gospel-present ministry by only preaching the narrow gospel, gospel-centered youth workers also build a culture that is shaped by the broader gospel. For a deeper examination of the gospel's impact on youth ministry, please see *Gospel-Centered Youth Ministry: A Practical Guide,* edited by Cameron Cole and Jon Nielson.[171]

---

[171]Cameron Cole and Jon Nielson, eds. *Gospel-Centered Youth Ministry: A Practical Guide* (Wheaton, IL: Crossway, 2016).

Chapter 8

Youth Ministry as a Bridge Between the Church and Home

Every weekend tourists and locals flood over one of two bridges to enjoy the beaches of Cape Cod. The traffic along the seven-mile-long Cape Cod Canal is inevitable because they are the only two ways in or out of Cape Cod. The bridges are important, but they are not the destination. While some bridges are indeed remarkable feats of architecture and engineering, a bridge is always a means to an end—in the case of the Bourne and Sagamore Bridges: a relaxing weekend with friends or family in a beautiful scenic beach community.

In the same way, a well-run and exciting youth group is never the point of youth ministry. The goal of youth ministry is not even to produce teenage Christians. Instead, the purpose of youth ministry is to produce *adult* disciples whose faith took root and was nourished throughout their teen years. Some of these adults first heard and responded to the gospel through the youth ministry, and some of them likely grew up in Christian families and in the church. Because the goal of youth ministry is far greater than the youth ministry itself, it is incumbent upon youth workers to keep their eyes fixed on the big picture.

There are many temptations for youth workers to lure them into building a ministry infrastructure to impress and entertain teenagers whose attention is increasingly difficult to capture, but this temptation must be resisted. When ministry to teenagers nurtures their faith without this bigger picture, their faith is often rooted in the youth group or parachurch ministry—only to be uprooted when they graduate and are forced to be replanted elsewhere. Often, however, these students' faith is simply uprooted and never transplanted into an ongoing relationship with a local church. In these cases, the youth ministry has not served as a bridge, but as the destination, and have left students as spiritual orphans.

Youth ministry serves as a faithful bridge to lifelong discipleship when it is an expression of meaningful partnership between the family and the local church. For those youth ministries who begin in sixth grade, they have eight years to make an impact on students. That is a long time, but those students will indeed leave the ministry eventually. And yet, barring any family breakdown, those same students' family relationships will remain. While youth workers have long advocated for the importance of partnership with parents, much of it has been mere lip-service. It is time for youth workers to finally commit to a genuine partnership with parents in ministry to the next generation.

In light of the above explorations of biblical foundations for youth ministry and the need to build upon the gospel, the following admissions and corresponding building-blocks provide some general applications that can guide youth workers to evaluate whether or not their ministry is functioning as a bridge or a destination.

Three Admissions

Youth Ministry is Temporary

This is the most obvious admission that is necessary, but is surprisingly overlooked by many youth workers: Youth ministry is for adolescence, the family is for life, and the Church is for eternity. Biblical-ly-minded youth workers remember this constantly because they view their ministry as bridge-building endeavor rather than as a destination. This does not diminish the value of youth ministry any more than the importance of the Bourne Bridge for those who are visiting Cape Cod for the weekend. Without those bridges, a weekend on the Cape simply wouldn't happen. Bridges are important and serve a bigger purpose than themselves: they exist to serve the people who need to move from one side of the river or chasm to the other. Similarly, youth ministry is never an end-in-itself.

It is important to clarify that by talking about youth ministry, this book is emphasizing the local church's particular ministry to teenagers. That ministry might be highly structured and involve multiple full-time ministers, or it could be very simple and volunteer run. What is most important is the church's commitment to provide an intentional min-istry of partnership with parents so teenagers would grow a lifelong faith in Jesus Christ. Churches are short-sighted and negligent of their calling to the next generation if they are capable of providing a well-equipped minister to the next generation but relegate that ministry to volunteers. Youth ministry is real pastoral ministry and should be over-seen by spiritually mature and doctrinally-sound leaders. Any church in which the pastoral staff and elders are disconnected from the youth ministry is in gross disobedience to the biblical mandate to raise up a faithful generation. In some ways, smaller churches have an advantage over larger churches in building a youth ministry as a bridge, because the youth ministry will not have the option of being completely void of parental and pastoral involvement. To continue the metaphor: the smaller the river, the smaller the bridge will need to be. Unfortunately, many small churches who cannot afford to pay anyone to lead a youth ministry often feel like failures. Instead, each church should prayer-fully bring the church leaders and the parents together to discuss and envision ways to minister to teenagers and to give them a meaningful role in the life of their church. Even if this may not provide many high energy game nights, it will give students a remarkable and invaluable sense of belonging that will serve them well.

Simply put, there comes a time when students are no longer allowed to attend youth group. This is why most ministries have a celebration for high school graduates: it is a rite of passage out of the youth ministry. Graduation marks a transitional season for students, but it ultimately means, "We still love you, but you don't belong here anymore." It is absolutely essential for faithful youth ministry leaders to prepare students for life after youth group.

Parents Matter More Than Youth Pastors Do

The exegetical, historical, and theological foundations for youth ministry continually affirm the responsibility parents have in their children's lives. Sociological studies continue to find the same thing: parents are the most significant influences in a teenager's life. Hopefully that influence is godly and positive, but in cases of abuse or neglect that influence is damaging and negative (but equally formative). The only times parents are not the lead-influencer in a teenager's life is when they have chosen to give that authority to someone else. Youth workers have an incredible ministry opportunity in the life of a teenager, but they simply cannot (and should not) replace the influence of parents.

If youth workers truly want to help students grow a lifelong faith, overlooking parents is not an option. In *Families and Faith*, Vern Bengtson unfolds the sociological data of a thirty-five year-long study of over 350 families over four generations. The oldest person surveyed was born as long ago as 1881 and the most recent was born in 1988. In summary of the research, Bengtson concludes,

1. Religious families are surprisingly successful at transmission.
2. Parental influence has not declined since the 1970s.
3. Parental warmth is the key to successful transmission.
4. Grandparents are more important than we recognize.
5. Interfaith marriage and divorce deter religious transmission.
6. Religious rebels, zealots, and prodigals are outcomes of non-transmission.
7. Religious "nones" are also products of intergenerational transmission.
8. High-boundary religious groups have high rates of transmission.
9. Generations differ in their perceptions of God and spirituality.[172]

The influence of parents is absolutely undeniable, and has not been marginalized in recent years. Parents remain central in their children's faith development, even if that faith is apathetic or opposed to religion. Among the most notable takeaways in Bengtson's study is the importance of "parental warmth," which is described as, "warm, affirming, and respectful."[173] Children who see and experience genuine care and love from their parents have an easier time receiving the care and love of God through Jesus Christ, while those whose parents are cold or harsh find themselves closing themselves off from the gospel. This simply accords with much of the biblical teaching presented in this book. To be clear, parental influence is not a reality because sociological research continues to affirm it. Parental influence is a God-ordained reality that is so undeniable that sociological studies continue to bear witness to it.

---

[172]Bengtson, *Families and Faith*, 184-92.
[173]Ibid, 80.

The biblical, historical, theological, and even sociological record is absolutely consistent: parents matter more than youth workers do. This absolutely does not mean youth workers have no influence and should be viewed simply as optional. Instead, it sets the perspective for youth workers who are frequently tempted to overstate their importance while criticizing parents as negligent. Because parents are largely determinative of their children's adult faith, youth workers would be wise to become the greatest advocate for the parents of their students—and when those parents are not Christians, it would certainly be a good investment of time and effort to minister to the parents just as much as to the students.

The Students Are Never "My Kids" (they are "Our Kids")

Youth workers, whether paid or volunteer, represent the church's faithfulness to their commitment to children and their families that are undertaken during infant dedication (or infant baptism, depending on the church's theological convictions). It is common for youth workers to talk about students as "my kids." When this is said out of affection for students or to merely distinguish one youth group from another when partnering in ministry with another church, it is a simple statement of relationship—"These students are in my ministry and I love them." But when it is said in a way that communicates to others in the church, "These kids are more mine than they are yours," it betrays a fundamental misunderstanding of the nature of biblical youth ministry. Youth ministry forges a special bond, and while it's certainly a term of endearment to call students "our kids," a spirit of possessiveness should be guarded against and is extremely unhealthy.

Because intergenerational ministry is difficult to fuel and sustain in a church, viewing students as "my kids" can implicitly communicate to the rest of the church, "stay away, they're mine." Youth workers serve teenagers on behalf of the church in a specific and focused way. Many church members view the youth workers as those who have been given responsibility for teenagers. Instead, they should be seen as representatives of the church's commitment to teens rather than as agents who have been delegated that full responsibility. The entire church makes a commitment to the next generation when children are dedicated or baptized, and it is right for the Lord and parents to hold the church community to it. In this way, as the family of God, the children of the church are truly "our kids," to whom the church family has pledged to minister.

After a lengthy research project examining churches who are exceptional in retaining the younger generations, one of the key findings from the Fuller Youth Institute was, "For young people today, relational warmth is the new cool."[174] Once again, as is the case with the family, "warmth" is the key. Churches who invest themselves, not just money, into ministry to students are those who reap the fruit. Youth workers who admit the teenagers are not "my kids" support parents while also advocating for students to be known, cared for, and involved in other areas of the church's life. The teenagers do not belong to the youth workers, they belong to the church community. This simply reflects the teachings already presented about biblical households and the Old Testament's emphasis on the community's responsibility to raise up the next generation in the fear and obedience of the Lord.

Three Essential Building-Blocks

Youth Ministry is Anchored to the Local Church

The Church is the Bride of Christ and the local church is God's plan for redemption. Families are important and parachurch ministries have a valuable supporting role, but the local church has a central

---

[174]Powell, *Growing Young*, 26.

place in the story of the Church. Once again, biblically faithful youth ministry is a bridge that helps students grow the roots of their faith in the soil of the local church. Teenagers who are explicitly or implicitly taught that participation in the local church is optional have a tendency to become adults with a subtle malaise toward the church. This has been the default setting from which most youth ministries have operated over the last century, and it has brought a current reality where church membership is increasingly viewed with suspicion. It is entirely possible to turn the local church into an idol, but the more common temptation in today's culture is one that turns the church into another marketplace competing for family's time and commitment. Instead of giving into the temptation to compete, families and ministries (whether church-based or parachurch) would be wise to seek opportunities to foster intergenerational discipleship and to meaningfully prepare students for a lifetime of participation in a church. Naturally, this is more complicated for parachurch ministries who risk showing favoritism to certain churches in the community by sending students to *Church A* and *Church B* but never to *Church C* or *D*. This is surely a sensitive matter, but one that should not deter parachurch youth workers from helping students find their place in a church.

Every church-based youth ministry will reflect the church in which it resides. For instance: a church that is weak in evangelism is fertile soil for a youth ministry that struggles in evangelism, while a church that is strong in Bible-teaching will likely foster a student ministry committed to expository teaching. In the cases where this similarity is not true, it is probable that the youth ministry is not functioning as a bridge, but as its own entity. In these instances, the church-based youth ministry is functionally a parachurch ministry funded and hosted by the local church. Occasionally, the Lord will spark revitalization in the broader church through the youth ministry; but it is entirely possible for a youth ministry to be *trying* to initiate this revitalization in ways that actually undermines the leadership and ministry of that church. When youth ministry is an expression of the church's mission, it will necessarily retain some of the DNA of the church at large. For this reason, youth workers ought to carefully align their ministry to prepare students for participation in the church. When non-Christian teenagers are converted through a youth ministry that is high energy and cutting edge, but then attend Sunday worship at that church to discover a traditional worship service, they will struggle to transition into church participation. In a very practical sense, the branding and social media presence of the youth ministry should be clearly aligned with the church's culture and personality.

Once again, the goal of youth ministry is not simply to produce teenage disciples, but to see teenagers become adult disciples who serve in the church out of a deep love for Jesus. Because this is the long-term goal of biblical youth ministry, it is counter-productive to minister to teenagers in a way that implicitly teaches them they can become mature Christians while remaining separated from the local church.

Be the Parents' Greatest Advocate

Returning to Bengtson's findings in *Families and Faith,* parents who are harsh or rigid in forcing religious conformity often produce religious "prodigals" or "rebels." Some children become prodigals, meaning they rejected their parents' faith but eventually returned at a later time. Regarding the Rebels, who have rejected their parents' faith and not returned, Bengtson explains, "Rebels came from strongly religious families where there was 'too much of a good thing,' as parents' religious socialization efforts were experienced as excessive or intrusive."[175] Interestingly, the study found that many parents who were prodigals have children who become rebels, presumably because they so desperately want to keep their children away from the heartache they them-

---

[175]Bengtson, *Families and Faith,* 142.

selves experienced during their prodigal years, they actually push their kids toward the very thing they fear.[176] Youth workers can be instrumental for parents when they have built up mutual trust and respect, to give warning when students are showing signs of becoming prodigals or rebels. It is common for parents to hear these warnings as a word of judgment ("You're pushing your kid away!") rather than as a legitimate concern by someone who is a true partner in ministry to their child. Unless youth workers have already raised teenagers, it would be wise to refrain from giving parenting advice. Instead, every youth worker can faithfully remind parents to the promises of Scripture while serving as a helpful guide to understanding youth culture.

The next era of youth ministry will require youth workers to grow in their commitment to parents as well as students. Youth workers cannot advocate for parents if they only have a relationship with the students. One practical temptation that most youth workers face arises when students share a behind the scenes story of "what it's really like" at home. Because of youth workers' love for students they are extremely prone to siding with students during a family conflict rather than remaining as a neutral party who can facilitate reconciliation and healing. Wisdom and experience guides youth workers to listen carefully, ask good questions, and intentionally pursue conversations with both the student and the parent. Again, this reflects the importance of open and respectful dialogue between parents and youth workers in order to embrace a commitment to co-discipleship with parents.

Most vocational youth ministers are young adults who, if they have children, are young parents. Because of their age and family experiences, youth ministers are rarely the best people in the church to actually disciple the parents of teenagers. And yet, in the midst of the busyness of local church ministry they may serve as parents' advocate among the

---

[176]Ibid, 143.

church leadership. During board meetings, staff meetings, and other leadership-level conversations, youth workers have the opportunity to keep parents and students on the minds of the "decision makers" of the church. When youth workers embrace their identity as an advocate for parents, it also guards against a posture of skepticism or mistrust. Instead, parents will view the youth minister as their pastor, not only their teenager's.

Beyond the ministry of the local church, it would be worthwhile for Christians who are burdened for the next generation to consider opportunities to serve parents in the community. When youth workers and church members serve on the school committee or coach in the town's soccer league, it fosters relationships with unchurched parents while investing in church families beyond the church property. Of course, there are sacrifices required to pursue these types of partnerships, but they are powerful displays of the individual and the church's commitment to families in the community. Christian parents are not the only ones who want what is best for their children. By coming alongside unchurched parents in order to serve their families, the love and compassion of God is made tangible to parents who probably view the church as aloof and unhelpful for anything except weddings and funerals.

Ultimately, the best pathway to become a youth ministry that bridges the church and home is not to discover the perfect program, but to foster a churchwide culture where families and the next generation are important. At its core, a church must build upon a biblical foundation as it seeks to minister to families. Excellent programming, when not built upon the gospel and a biblical vision for co-discipleship with parents, will not produce the lasting fruit among teenagers anyone desires. However, ministry to students that intentionally partners with parents to proclaim the gospel and to help students understand the transforming power of the grace of God, will bear much fruit (even if the programming is fairly basic and run completely by volunteers). In a small church that type of partnership may be overseen by the pastor and volunteers, but in medium and larger churches there will likely be pastoral staff to oversee this ministry. May the coming generation of youth workers return once again to the biblical, historical, and theological foundations for ministry to students by advocating for families and promoting a vision for co-evangelism and co-discipleship of teenagers.

Create Moments for Parents and Youth to Be Together

One of the great tragedies of the modern church is found on Sunday mornings when families arrive for worship and split into separate programs, only to join together again in the parking lot on their way home. In the midst of increasing busyness and time-constraints on family life, church should be a place where families are drawn together by the Word of God. As the previous chapters explored, there is biblical precedent for the freedom to speak to only certain ages at a time and for very young children to be in the nursery or childcare during gathered worship, but the church must be intergenerational.

Parents often struggle to find moments where they can bond with their children at church, especially during the teen years. One of the more common experiences Christian parents have with their teenagers is "forcing" them to attend church and youth group. Arguing all morning and rushing out the door to arrive five minutes late for worship hardly qualifies as a positive church experience together, but this is a common experience for many families.

When youth workers are planning their ministry calendar, it would be a great blessing to families to plan an occasional activity that brings families together to create positive memories at church. This honors the family, includes parents, and can even help teenagers see another side of their own parents. There are many activities that can be used to create meaningful times for families: painting nights, cooking competitions, board games, instructional events where different skills can be taught,[177] or a Family-Feud type of showdown. For those nights when families would compete as a team against one another, students whose parents are absentees, unengaged, or simply unable to attend can be "adopted" into a new family by adults from the congregation who volunteer to be foster parents for the night. As cliché as it may be, including parents as drivers and hosts for youth ministry activities is another way to invite them into the flow of ministry and to demonstrate that what happens at youth group is not private.

Because the local church is a living expression of the Church as the family of God, creating opportunities for families to grow in their faith *together* should be a regular priority for the church leadership (not only for the youth workers). Creating space for families to bond, to laugh, and to experience meaningful times together is a practical outworking of viewing youth ministry as a bridge between the church and the home. Giving parents and teenagers positive experiences together help strengthen the bond that should exist between the student, parent, and church.

Practical Counsel on Becoming a Bridge-Building Youth Ministry

Transitioning to become a bridge-building youth ministry is a significant paradigm shift, especially for veteran youth workers with established ministries. As with most change, the larger the scale of one's ministry, the more difficult transition will be and the longer it will take. With this in mind, the following are hard-learned lessons to provide guidance in the journey toward a bridge-building youth ministry that

---

[177]I know churches who have hosted sessions like, "How to change your oil," "How to do the laundry" (especially for graduating seniors before they leave for college), and others when teenagers taught the adults various computer/technology skills.

is in line with the biblical, historical, and theological foundations presented in earlier chapters.

Think Big, Start Small

This is the most practical advice a leader can receive when he or she is beginning a new chapter of leadership. During a season of new discoveries and reinvigorated passion for ministry, many leaders have been disheartened by others' lack of vision and complacency. Youth workers who are entering this transition should remember how long it took them to arrive at their newfound convictions, and to be patient with their volunteer team and parents. Often, the point of frustration arose from others being either overwhelmed by the grandeur of the new vision, or the actual steps toward accomplishing that vision were never clearly defined. It is good and right for churches to have a big vision for their youth ministries.

When a church is content for the youth ministry to remain in the youth room and views their calling to teenagers as being fulfilled by the designated youth workers, this transition will take more time—especially since a church in this condition is composed of parents who are largely unengaged. The wise youth pastor will think big but start small by finding a few likeminded allies in the church and then pursuing easy victories. This approach follows the same line of thought as the "debt snowball," where smaller debts are paid off first to roll the lower payments into the larger debts. Celebrating smaller victories earns youth worker credibility and provides encouragement to continue the leadership transition while also opening up talking-points with other church members and parents about the bigger picture that is being pursued. This approach also gives small foretastes of what is being pursued, making the bigger vision more understandable to those who are still trying to understand where this transition may lead.

Prioritize Engaged Parents

In the same line of thought as "think big, start small," it is good and right to desire each parent to play an increasingly significant role in ministry to teenagers in the church, but no one begins with that reality. Prioritize those who are interested or already on board. Every youth worker who has hosted a "Parent's Night" will report that most parents who attend are those who needed to attend the least, meanwhile those who never attend a parents meeting are those who need them most. Rather than focusing on reaching the unreachable, begin with those who are interested and teachable, then deputize them as ambassadors to the rest of the parents. When youth workers spend their time and energy trying to reach parents who are distant and unresponsive, frustration and discouragement will surely follow. Beginning with those parents who are most receptive will create a small group to serve as a model for other parents to actually see the bridge-building vision at work in their friend's families.

It is wonderful to want every parent and every family in the church to get on board with family discipleship and meaningful co-discipleship with the church, but this is simply unrealistic. Every church will always have some parents who are unengaged and spiritually negligent of their calling to family discipleship. Rather than being a rejection of everything else written in this book, this is a recognition of real life in a healthy church who is welcoming new Christians and unchurched teenagers. These new Christians will need to be mentored by other parents in order to catch the vision for family discipleship, while non-Christian parents will generally be happy to have their kids keep busy in a safe place with positive adult role models. If half of the parents in one's church are practicing family discipleship, this should be considered a great victory. As the ministry progresses and church members grow in Christian maturity, not only should the unengaged become engaged in family worship, but they should also be inviting and evangelizing their non-Christians friends and family out of obedience to the Great Commission. In this way, the need for promoting family discipleship is always ongoing.

Finally, prioritizing engaged parents requires constant effort because new parents enter the ministry every year when their children enter the youth ministry. Youth workers can easily feel like a broken record who grow tired of saying the same thing over and over, but this is a necessary commitment to bridge-building with parents. Hopefully this bridge-building is not unique to the youth ministry but is a church-wide value. When this church-wide emphasis is present, parents will need the leader's help to know what partnership during the teen years will look like. Once again, this is where prioritizing receptive parents is most important—not only will new parents in the ministry hear from the youth leaders what partnership entails, they will also see it modeled by fellow parents who they can turn to for encouragement and support.

Pursue Allies in Senior Leadership

The youth pastor who catches a vision for church-wide partnerships but lacks the full support of the church's senior leadership, will soon discover a fairly low ceiling for bridge-building. This unfortunate reality has been the story for many youth workers who desire to see parents and the church meaningfully co-disciple the next generation only to be met with verbal agreement from senior leaders but without any further involvement beyond, "Yes, great idea." The reason for this relatively low ceiling has a few causes. First, youth pastors are generally given little authority regarding the church's ministry beyond the teenagers. Second, the senior leaders have many responsibilities to oversee and often feel the weight of leadership for all ministries in the church, not only the youth and children's ministry. Especially if the youth ministry is being well-led, their distance is often an expression of trust rather than lack of care. Third, meaningfully implementing a church-wide commitment to bridge-building and co-discipleship requires these commitments to seep into the DNA of every ministry of the church. This takes significant time and effort. If this vision is seen as a program or simply another thing to do, it will fall by the wayside as an item on the agenda that keeps getting overlooked for more pressing matters. But when senior leaders catch the vision for co-evangelism and co-discipleship of the next generation they will begin to speak this vision into the leaders of the church's ministries.

Rather than starting a new program, work with the senior leadership to coach existing ministries to embrace a vision for equipping parents to minister to their kids. In the same way that small group leaders ask, "How does this apply at work?" they will also ask, "How could this change the way you talk to your kids the next time they misbehave or embarrass you?" or "How could you teach this to your children?" Some might object that not every adult is a parent so it is inappropriate to make such applications, and yet small group leaders routinely apply Scripture to marriage and work when not every attendee is married or employed. This is simply one example of the trickle down from senior leadership's commitment to bridge-building that a youth pastor cannot bring about without them.

When given opportunities to attend meetings with senior leaders, take them. Do not view these meetings as time away from student ministry, but recognize the potential for raising the ceiling for family discipleship. Resist the temptation of only talking about students and parents. Seek to meaningfully contribute to conversations about the topics at hand. Demonstrating competency and wisdom will go far in showing trustworthiness and leadership when youth and family ministries are discussed.

When youth leaders are discouraged because their leadership has either rejected the vision for bridge-building or given lip-service to it, the best response is to lead by example. It might seem obvious and unnecessary to state, but demonstrating the change one wants to see is often the best way to get others on board. As opportunities arise to discuss what is happening in the ministry, prioritize the stories of model families and invite them to share with fellow parents and with senior leaders about the bridge-building vision.

It must also be stated that this may be a valid and healthy reason to leave a church. There are times when a significant change in ministry philosophy will cause enough friction between the youth pastor and the church leadership that it is best for both parties to separate from each other. Seek counsel and do not be hasty, but it may be better to resign and find a new church than to continually breed conflict and division.

Build a Team Who Shares the Vision

Every good leader knows they need a strong team. For those youth workers who read this book and desire to transition their ministry to become a bridge-building youth ministry, the youth leadership team will be pivotal. If there are members who resist this vision and are not enthusiastic about developing meaningful partnerships with parents, it will be better in the long-run to remove them from the ministry as graciously as possible than it would be to keep them on the team while trying to simultaneously persuade them and implement a new vision. Perhaps these leaders could take a sabbatical while they consider the new vision for the ministry.

Once again, discerning leaders will think big but start small. This means the youth leadership team must be given sufficient time to study, discuss, and prayerfully reflect on what this bridge-building will look like in their church and in their ministry with their particular students and parents. Enacting a significant change in ministry philosophy too quickly can easily lead to either conflict or false-agreement among volunteers who do not want to leave the students in their ministry, but are unconvinced of the changes that are being promoted by the youth pastor. It would be helpful to take a year to read through this book together with one's leadership team prior to making any significant changes in the youth ministry.

Open and honest conversations about change are vital. Therefore, leaders need to lead while also creating space for honest questioning and push-back. This can sometimes lead to uncertainty and tension and must be well-managed to prevent a walking-on-eggshells atmosphere among the leadership team; however, these conversations are crucial to lead the ministry into a bridge-building youth ministry.

Do a Few Things Consistently

One of the greatest temptations for those who have newly caught this vision is to go overboard in their effort to build the bridge overnight. Rather than planning various programs or seminars for parents and families, start with just one and run it twice per year, every year for the next decade. Here's why: Parents are busy and overloaded. Many already feel like failures and they know they should take a greater role in the spiritual development of their teen, but they don't know how so they trust the church to primarily do it for them. Suddenly being invited to various church efforts seems both overwhelming and guilt-inducing. Wondering, "What if people find out I haven't read the Bible with my kid in years?" will keep many parents out of the conversation. There may have been an occasional reminder to pray with your teen and to talk about the gospel with him or her, but to suddenly be invited to regular family discipleship events and seminars can be a shock to parents who are already overwhelmed. When there is a lackluster response and involvement from parents, hosting one parents' night twice per year provides consistency and familiarity while allowing those parents who have attended to invite and reach out to those who are hesitant. One regular effort, when repeated enough, becomes familiar enough and is eventually viewed as another integral part of the youth ministry's partnership with parents and may become a catalyst for greater partnership in the future. This slow and consistent effort will eventually build a solid foundation upon with a more meaningful and regular partnership can be built.

A Final Word to Church Leaders, Youth Workers, and Parents of Teenagers

Youth ministry has consistently verbalized the importance of partnering with parents while building a structure that effectively left them out. That is changing and youth workers are recognizing their role as bridge-builders between the church and the home. In the end, the solution is not to have more or better programs. What is necessary is a DNA shift within the broader Church that is centered around a recommitment to co-evangelizing and co-discipling the next generation in the gospel of grace. When students come home and when they come to church, may they find gospel prompted warmth that sprouts into lifelong faithfulness to Jesus Christ.

This next era of youth ministry looks bright. May it be built upon a gospel-centered biblical theology that affirms the role of teenagers in the Church and in the church.

Epilogue
The Bare Minimums of a Biblical Youth Ministry

After reading *A Biblical Theology of Youth Ministry*, a common question may be: "So What? What are the bare minimums that must be present for a youth ministry to be faithful to Scripture?" The purpose of this epilogue is not to present more research, but to share some brief, final conclusions. Whereas the Five Pillars of Gospel Centered Youth Ministry (see chapter seven) are meant to present a more robust portrait about how the gospel shapes youth ministry; this brief epilogue is meant to give the bare minimums that every youth ministry, regardless of paradigm or cultural context, must adhere to in order to be in line with Scripture.

Parents First

Youth workers are important and play a crucial role in the lives of teenagers, but they must never replace the spiritual priority of parents. Instead, they are called to come alongside parents as co-evangelists and co-disciplers of the next generation. Students whose parents display genuine faith and relational warmth are far more likely to continue in the faith through adulthood than students who attend every youth group event throughout high school but whose parents are spiritually passive. When parents are not discipled themselves, they are left unequipped to be the spiritual leaders their children so desperately need. This is disappointingly common. In these cases, and in those families where the parents are not Christians, the youth worker may serve as the parents' best advocate to mobilize others in the church to disciple the parents. In some extreme cases, youth workers might want to consider spending less time with students in order to encourage and minister to the parents. As counter-intuitive as that may seem, it may pay a long-term dividend in the life of every family member. While the priority of parents has long been a stated value of youth ministry, it is time for partnership with parents to become an actual priority for youth workers.

Worship Together

Churches who provide a separate "worship experience" for students during the church's gathered worship time are in clear disregard of the biblical worship. Throughout the Old Testament, New Testament, and even throughout Church History, the generations worshipped together. The liturgy often carried an emphasis on passing down the faith from generation to generation, which obviously necessitated the generations to actually be together. This intergenerational priority does not demand complete elimination of all age-specific ministries, but it does require two things: first, that children who are old enough to learn and understand are present, and second, that those who plan the worship service to keep children in mind as they prepare. While discipleship may take place in varied contexts, the generations belong together during the church's gathered worship.

The Church Must Commit to Discipleship

The last century of modern youth ministry has shown that youth workers have employed effective strategies to get kids to attend their ministries. But the last century also shows that simply isn't enough. It hasn't worked. Rather than obsessing on increasing attendance, the church should begin to focus on retention, and that requires a renewed commitment to discipleship. When a ministry prioritizes discipleship, evangelism must also be emphasized, for one of the central elements of discipleship is equipping students for evangelism.

In Scripture and throughout history, discipleship of the next generation was never the task of the select few. It has always been a community-project. The entire clan would share in passing down the faith to the next generation. The faith community would support parents in their discipleship efforts and would sponsor children throughout their catechetical journey. Pastors would often meet with the adolescents for Bible Studies. These were not tasks delegated to the spiritually immature or to those who were only a few years older than the students themselves – they were high callings that were prioritized by the spiritual leaders of the community. Therefore, a church should view discipleship as the primary purpose of youth ministry rather than viewing it as a safe and entertaining place for church kids to be sheltered from the world.

The Gospel Always

Youth Ministry does not exist to help students get into National Honor Societies or into a great college. It doesn't even exist to help students become well behaved citizens. The biblical purpose of youth ministry is to make lifelong disciples of the next generation. Whether they are church kids or vocally opposed to religion, faithful youth workers serve with a commitment to announce the good news of Jesus Christ to teenagers. Rather than allowing for an "evangelism or discipleship" debate, gospel-centered youth workers seek to help students receive the grace of Jesus Christ through the *narrow gospel* while discipling students into a biblical worldview through teaching the *broader gospel*. At the end of the day, youth ministry must resist the temptation to have a "try harder" approach that can only produce behavior-modification, and must instead adopt a grace-driven obsession that points students to the love of God through Jesus Christ.

Final Conclusion

It is a daring thing for a youth pastor to honestly ask the question, "Is my youth ministry biblical?" Because if the answer is "No," there will be a troubling dilemma. On one hand, ignoring the conflict does not seem like a viable option. But on the other hand, making the necessary changes can lead to conflict with church leadership, parents, or other youth workers who think everything is fine the way it is. Conviction requires courage. The difference between conviction and arrogance is humility. If you have read this book and are struggling with a few areas where you see the need for alignment, revisit chapter 8's counsel to "think big, start small." Lead with humble conviction and look for easy victories, stacking them on top of each other in order to build momentum. And consider reading this book (or portions of it) with a team so you aren't leading alone. Finally, and I have experienced this myself, if your convictions about the way youth ministry should be done leads you to conflict with others—be gracious and kind, for you didn't always see youth ministry this way either. But stand upon the Word of God, holding true to your convictions. Upon what other foundation should you build?

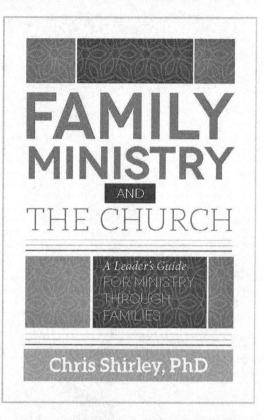

What if
what happened here

Also
happened here

D6
CURRICULUM

D6 connects the church and home through *generational discipleship.*

A family-aligned curriculum for every generation!

D6FAMILY.COM

Based on Deuteronomy 6:5-9

D6 | CONFERENCE

a family ministry conference
connecting CHURCH and HOME
through generational discipleship

D6conference.com